THE OPEN UNIVERSITY

Arts: A Third Level Course
A361 SHAKESPEARE

BLOCK IV

Hamlet

Prepared for the Course Team by Roger Day

The Open University Press

The Open University Press
Walton Hall, Milton Keynes
MK7 6AA

First published 1984

Designed by the Graphic Design Group of the Open University.

Printed in Great Britain by
Albert Gait Limited
Grimsby

ISBN 0 335 11214 5

This text forms part of an Open University course. The complete list of units in
the course appears on the back cover of this text.

For general availability of supporting material referred to in this text, please write to
Open University Educational Enterprises Limited, 12 Cofferidge Close,
Stony Stratford, Milton Keynes, MK11 1BY, Great Britain.

Further information on Open University courses may be obtained from the
Admissions Office, The Open University, PO Box 48, Walton Hall, Milton Keynes,
MK7 6AB.

1.1

Contents

Hamlet

Study Material

The study material for Block IV consists of the following:

THE CORRESPONDENCE TEXTS

TELEVISION*

| Programme 5 | *Hamlet* 'workshop' (1) |
| Programme 7 | *Hamlet* 'workshop' (2) |

AUDIO CASSETTES

Cassette 1 — Shakespeare's Theatre
(a number of examples are taken from *Hamlet*)

Cassette 3, side B — *Hamlet*: the text and the actors

Cassette 6(p), side A — Performance extract (15 minutes approx.) (See Cassette Notes for details. The scenes played have been chosen to illustrate in part the study of the language of the play, this block, pages 31–40.)

RADIO

Programme 4 — *Hamlet*: a play for all times (in which reasons are discussed for the appeal of *Hamlet* to different ages and cultures)

* *Note.* The emphasis in the block is largely on the *text* of the play. The purpose of the TV 'workshop' programmes is to illustrate and explore how interpretations of particular scenes can vary, quite legitimately, when the play becomes alive in performance in the theatre. There is a useful paperback, *Hamlet: Text and Performance* by Peter Davison, Macmillan, 1983, which discusses both the staging of the play and the history of its performances in the theatre and on film.

Introduction

AMLET is the longest of Shakespeare's plays and simply reading it with the degree of attention appropriate to this course will take a fair proportion of the time allocated to this block. The New Penguin edition was chosen partly because it is a pleasant text to use and partly because of the excellent introductory essay by Anne Barton to which I shall be referring and which I shall ask you to read. Because this constitutes a lot of reading, there is no other critical material provided in this block, though a great deal is readily available should you want to explore further at a later date (see page 56 of the set text, 'Further Reading').

Hamlet is probably the most widely known of Shakespeare's plays (I shall be considering why this is so) and the old joke that it is 'full of quotations' reveals how widespread is familiarity with at least some of the play's lines and speeches. This can be a hindrance rather than a help to the student attempting to form a view of it, for frequent 'recognition' disrupts the attention which less celebrated but equally important and interesting parts of the play deserve. So I would suggest that even (or perhaps especially) if you have seen and/or read *Hamlet* many times, you read *all* of it again, making notes on aspects which strike or perhaps puzzle you. There is a helpful explanatory 'Commentary' at the back of the set text but, given the play's length and the time available, it is more important to develop a familiarity with it as a whole and with its structure than to puzzle over some of the more obscure phrases. You will probably have time for only one complete detailed reading though I shall be directing your attention to particular scenes and asking you to look at them again in more detail. (A reason, incidentally, for having *Hamlet* nearer the end of the course is that you will have developed some familiarity with reading Shakespearean verse by this point and should be able to read it more easily.)

Before you begin to read, I would like to suggest several ideas which are central to any discussion of the play and which you might bear in mind as you move through it.

(1) What is the play 'about'? That is, what *kind* of play is it: the tragedy of an individual; 'Revenge' tragedy; a political and historical drama?

(2) To what extent is it legitimate to discuss the character of Hamlet independently of the dramatic action? And how is it possible to do this?

(3) What moral judgements, if any, are implied in the play, particularly towards the taking of revenge?

(4) How helpful is it to compare *Hamlet* with *Antony and Cleopatra* or *King Lear* as tragedy?

I shall return to these questions later, but I would like to remind you at the outset that in considering them there is one particularly important fact to remember. There is a sense in which each production of any play is unique (because of different actors, settings, etc.) but in the case of *Hamlet* this is especially true because, first, the modern, printed text is so long (taking nearly four or five hours to perform) that in almost all productions certain parts are cut according to the director's view of the play. Secondly, there are various ways of producing and editing the play because of the variant texts. That is to say, your answer to the questions posed above will depend to some extent on the evidence provided by a particular producer or editor. Two brief examples will illustrate this. Jan Kott, the Polish critic, describes a production he saw in his own country:*

---

* Kott, J. (1964) '*Hamlet* of the Mid-Century' in his *Shakespeare Our Contemporary*, Methuen.

The *Hamlet* produced in Cracow a few weeks after the Twentieth Congress of the Soviet Communist Party lasted exactly three hours. It was light and clear, tense and sharp, modern and consistent, limited to one issue only. It was a political drama *par excellence*. 'Something is rotten in the state of Denmark'—was the first chord of Hamlet's new meaning . . .

. . . Doubtless it was a simplified *Hamlet*. But it is equally certain that this interpretation was so suggestive that when I reached for the text after the performance, I saw in it only a drama of political crime.

You might reasonably ask why reaching for the text failed to correct the view that *Hamlet* was 'only a drama of political crime' although it is not difficult to see how persuasive a version edited for production in a certain way could be; in this instance one dictated by overtly ideological considerations. At the other extreme is the version that William Hazlitt created for himself as a reader in 1817:

[Hamlet] is the prince of philosophical speculators . . . His ruling passion is to think, not to act . . .

. . . We do not like to see our author's plays acted and least of all, *Hamlet*. There is no play that suffers so much in being transferred to the stage . . . [Hamlet] is, as it were, wrapped up in his reflections, and only thinks aloud . . . He is full of weakness and melancholy, but there is no harshness in his nature. He is the most amiable of misanthropes.

(from Hazlitt, W. (1817) *Characters of Shakespeare's Plays*)

How could Kott and Hazlitt be writing about the same play? One explanation lies in the richness and variety it offers reader and director, thus enabling them to select the aspects which most appeal—intrigue and struggles for power to a politically aware critic in a country with a communist government, introspection and melancholy to a nineteenth-century man of letters. And there are weighty bibliographies to illustrate how many other views of the play have been put forward over the centuries. What I shall try to do in the main part of this block is to encourage you, by constant reference to the set text, to come to your own view which does not have to be as extreme or as over-simplified as either of those quoted.

Texts, sources and conventions

THE textual history of *Hamlet* is complex because there are three basic versions of the play, the First Quarto, the Second Quarto and the First Folio. Most editors choose to use the Second Quarto as the foundation of their edition with additions and emendations as appropriate from the First Quarto and the First Folio and this is one reason why the printed text is so long. If you are interested in the problems posed in editing, you will find 'An Account of the Text' on page 362 of your edition followed by lists collating (selectively) the variants. For present purposes, however, it is sufficient simply to be reminded that interpretation of particular parts of the play *may* be affected by the presence or absence of a speech. (The whole of IV.4, for example, does not appear in the First Folio, thus removing one of Hamlet's soliloquies.)

Sources and conventions are in fact connected, for the term 'convention' can be understood in relation to *Hamlet* in two ways. Usually it means an agreed way of doing something (as, for example, writing an elegy or composing a symphony) and in this sense Shakespeare's audience would readily have understood *Hamlet* as a 'tragedy of revenge'. I shall have more to say on this subject later when I come to consider the moral questions raised by the play, so for the present I shall simply give a brief outline of the kind of expectations it would have aroused. Common features of plays of this kind were that the murdered person to be avenged appeared in the form of a ghost to urge on the avenger (for example, Chapman's *The Revenge of Bussy D'Ambois*, *c.* 1610); madness, real or feigned, often afflicted the avenger (for example, Hieronimo in Kyd's *The Spanish Tragedy*, 1592); the revenge was occasioned because justice was not possible by legal means (for example, *Hamlet*). So from the very beginning of the play, an Elizabethan audience, even if they hadn't seen an earlier but now lost 'Hamlet', would be expecting what follows—delays in the protagonists's plans, a counter-plot by his intended victim and finally the death of the avenger himself. These are only some of the common characteristics of this kind of play for, though I refer to it as a convention, there weren't any definite rules to be kept to.

Shakespeare's *Hamlet* is also an example of a convention in the different sense of being (probably) based on an earlier Elizabethan play which would have been known to many of the public. It is important to grasp these facts because, as we shall see, the originality and vitality of the play come, in large measure, from the way in which Shakespeare exploits (and goes beyond) the expectations familiar conventions create. (In a similar fashion, Tom Stoppard's modern play *Rosencrantz and Guildenstern Are Dead* relies on an audience's familiarity with *Hamlet*.)

Interpreting the play

MORE has been written on *Hamlet* than any other play in the history of literature and, although much of it is repetitious, the volume of commentary indicates the fierce controversies discussion of it arouses. It's neither feasible nor desirable to investigate even a proportion of this literature in any detail in this block so I shall advert to some of it briefly when it seems appropriate to the discussion and then consider some in more detail later. I have already touched on one controversial point in putting Jan Kott beside Hazlitt in my introduction, and the questions raised by the enormous disparity of their views are really two of those I suggested that you should consider during your reading of the play, namely:

(1) What is the play 'about'?

(2) To what extent is it legitimate to discuss the character of Hamlet independently of the dramatic action?

To seek an answer to them, I suggest that you now turn to the text and read the play through carefully. You might find it useful to make a brief summary of what *actually happens* in each scene as this will be the basis of my discussion. (It will also be a useful reference aid in connecting one event with another.) I would like you in the course of reading to consider the comments and questions posed in the following pages, for they are designed to examine the function of particular scenes and to suggest points of particular interest. Then, before going on to the main discussion of the play, I would like you to read Anne Barton's 'Introduction' which will provide information about the sources of the play and the historical circumstances in which it was written, as well as offering a perceptive, well-argued view of the text.

NOW
READ THE
PLAY

Commentary and exercises

Title

The play is a 'tragedy' which, roughly speaking, would have signified to an Elizabethan audience the death of a highly placed person. We are reminded of Hamlet's rank and position.

Act I scene 1

Notice the unease created by the cold and by Francisco's melancholy, 'I am sick at heart' (l. 9), prior to the apparition. No view is expressed as to whether the spirit is 'good' or 'bad' ('erring' l. 155 means 'wandering'). The purpose of the scene is to sketch the political situation and to set the apparition within this: to Barnardo the latter is a 'portentous' figure (l. 109), to Horatio an omen (l. 134).

Act I scene 2

Claudius's first speech is studied in detail later in this block (p. 32) and is also on the performance cassette 6(p), side A. Hamlet's soliloquy (l. 129) is also on the same performance cassette. In addition, it is performed in the 'workshop' TV Programme 5: you might like to compare the interpretations.

Notice how (a) the theme of the state of the nation is continued (l. 9); (b) Laertes (whom Claudius addresses by his Christian name) is implicitly compared with Hamlet; and (c) Hamlet's melancholy is linked with disgust at his mother's remarriage—the theme of sexuality is introduced.

At this point, Hamlet only suspects 'some foul play' (l. 256).

Which of the interpretations of this part of the scene suggested in TV Programme 5 seems most plausible to you?

Act I scene 3

What is the function of this scene?

Surely

(1) To raise questions about the state of feelings between Hamlet and Ophelia—does he love her or is he pretending because of lust? Notice how the sexual theme is continued.

(2) To remind the audience of Hamlet's importance to the state of the country ('on his choice depends/The safety and health of this whole state' (ll. 20–1).

Note, too, the style of Polonius's advice (consistent with his role as Councillor of State); what more do we learn of Laertes—is his view of Hamlet overly suspicious, or properly circumspect?

Act I scene 4

What do we *learn* in this scene?

That

(1) Under Claudius the nation is becoming drunken and 'traduced' and that Hamlet cares about this.

(2) Hamlet believes in the immortality of the soul (l. 67).

(3) The ghost could be from either 'heaven' or 'hell'.

Notice the stress on human 'reason' (ll. 28 and 73) and compare with I.2.150.

Act I scene 5

What change do we see in Hamlet, and why?

Hamlet, moved by the revelations, becomes *resolved*. Revenge is a duty (l. 7) though the form it should take is not specified (l. 84). Notice the continued emphasis on lust (ll. 45, 54, 55 and 83) and on the state of the nation (l. 188).

NB Hamlet still isn't positive about the identity of the ghost—'honest' (l. 138) means 'genuine', not 'truthful'.

Act II scene 1

NB There is an interval of some months between the last scene and this one (see page 243 of the set text).

What is the principal *function* of this scene? What is its predominant *mood*?

Its function in the action is to show Hamlet preparing for his revenge by the assumption of his 'antic disposition'. Paradoxically, the mood is actually mainly comic, though the humour of Polonius's elaborate spying schemes turns blacker in the description of Hamlet's lunacy.

Act II scene 2

Part of this scene is performed in TV Programme 7.

This is a long scene—which parts of it contribute most directly to moving the action forward?

The political references to Fortinbras and his changed purpose 'against the Polack' are necessary for the ending of the play and continue the 'state of the nation' theme.

The soliloquy at the end of the scene is obviously important—Hamlet appears unable to explain his failure to act but gives as his reason doubt about the ghost's identity, though the 'melancholy' he has described earlier seems equally likely to be a reason. Note the continued references to sexual disgust (ll. 231–5).

What of the long section on the theatre and the players? What bearing might it have on the 'main action' in terms of 'playing a part'? Notice the humour in this scene—Hamlet's guying of Polonius, Polonius's 'witty' exchanges.

Act III scene 1

Part of this scene is on the performance cassette 6(p), side A.
This is known as the 'nunnery' scene, so-called because of Hamlet's rejection of Ophelia.

I suggest you bear two things in mind while reading this scene: (a) in what ways might it be played (given what little we know of Hamlet's true feelings for Ophelia); and (b) how is Hamlet's 'lunacy' relevant?

There are no stage directions or indications of tone of voice so we have to infer the appropriate way to play the scene from what has gone before. (How is it done on the cassette?) It is possible to see Hamlet in this scene as simply harshly dismissive but such a view is not consonant with either what we have seen of his character earlier or with the soliloquy at the beginning of the scene ('To be, or not to be . . . '). I find it more convincing to see Hamlet displaying a mixture of emotions in this scene, amongst which is genuine feeling for Ophelia. As to my question (b), remember that Hamlet does not display his 'antic disposition' in this scene and Claudius's judgement seems right (l. 164 ff.). Notice how Hamlet's outburst is against women in general ('you' and 'your' l. 143 ff. refer to all women, not just Ophelia).

Act III scene 2

Part of this scene I consider in detail later on.

What is the critical feature of this scene?

That Claudius's guilt (which he has admitted in an aside in III.1) is confirmed for Hamlet by his reaction to the play (l. 295). Notice how Hamlet's lewd remarks to Ophelia are at least partly a continuation of the 'lunacy' he displayed to her earlier.

Act III scene 3

Notice how the political theme of the play is touched on by Rosencrantz in his speech on the relationship between the good of the nation and that of its King (l. 11 ff.)—you might compare this with Hamlet's use of the royal 'we' in the previous scene (l. 340), the only occasion in the play when he employs it. You might consider too how Hamlet's stated reason for not killing Claudius reflects on himself.

Engraving of 'The Play Scene' (Act III, scene 2) in Hamlet. *Engraving by C. Rolls, from a painting by Daniel Maclise* (*Photo: The Raymond Mander & Joe Mitchenson Theatre Collection*)

Act III scene 4

This is the 'closet' scene which some see as the turning-point in the play.

Why might it be considered so?

Because in it Hamlet confronts his mother (who admits her guilt) and does take action (however mistakenly). This scene brings out clearly how dangerous Hamlet's position is. Notice how Hamlet sees himself as an instrument of providence (l. 174) and declares that he is *not* mad (l. 188). You might think about how the sexual revulsion in his address to his mother relates to his treatment of Ophelia.

Act IV scenes 1, 2 and 3

These scenes bring out the sense of a trap closing round Hamlet, equalled by his mistrust of his companions. Notice Claudius's reason for not acting publicly against Hamlet—'He's lov'd of the distracted multitude' ('distracted' means 'irrational').

Act IV scene 4

Part of this scene is studied later in this block and it is also performed both on the cassette and in TV Programme 7.

What does this scene, and the soliloquy in particular, contribute to our sense of Hamlet's progression in thought as the play moves forward?

Mainly it enacts the conflict he feels and attempts to analyse the tension between his position as a prince, bound to a duty of 'honour' and his inexplicable inability to take action. Notice, again, the emphasis on the uniquely human possession of 'reason' (l. 38).

Act IV scene 5

How does this scene provide another perspective on Hamlet? How is the pace of the action changing?

Stemming from Polonius's death, we learn of civil unrest and the people's desire for Laertes to be King (in an elective monarchy) in lines 104 and 108. When Laertes resolves to revenge his father's death, the comparison with Hamlet is brought out clearly. The action generally is gathering speed and, with the madness of Ophelia and the return of Laertes, moving to a climax. Notice the sexually suggestive songs Ophelia sings in her madness.

Act IV scenes 6 and 7

Part of scene 7 is performed in TV Programme 7.

How is the comparison between Hamlet and Laertes developed?

In terms of their attitude to revenge—compare Laertes's willingness to murder in church (IV.7.125) with Hamlet's earlier refusal to kill Claudius. Also, Hamlet, like Laertes, is popular with the people (IV.7.18).

Act V scene 1

What do the gravedigger's 'witty' exchanges with Hamlet remind you of? And what do we learn of Hamlet's feelings for Ophelia and attitude to Laertes?

The gravedigger is playing linguistic games with Hamlet just as Hamlet has himself done with others earlier (an explanation of this is offered in the Introduction to the set text, page 47). Hamlet states that he *did* love Ophelia (l. 265) and that he has a genuine respect for Laertes (l. 220), though he has himself assumed the title of ruler—'This is I/Hamlet the Dane' (ll. 253–4).

Act V scene 2

Part of this scene is performed in TV Programme 7. Another part is studied in detail later in this block (p.38) and is performed on Cassette 6(p), side A.

Has Hamlet's state of mind changed in any significant way by the time this final scene is reached? And what important points are made about rights to the throne and the succession? Finally, what kinds of reaction does the concluding slaughter invite?

Hamlet has progressed towards a more tranquil state of mind by the final scene. After his outburst against his mother in the 'closet' scene, the brooding on sexual impurity no longer preoccupies his thinking and the emphasis is now on the workings of providence (ll. 10 and 213). Although he lies to Laertes in saying that he killed Polonius while mad (assuming that by 'madness' he means the 'antic disposition' and not 'melancholy') his attitude essentially is one of respect to him and he sees the parallel between their positions (l. 76).

As to the right to the throne, Hamlet (whom Horatio addresses as someone regal) tells how Claudius took the throne after his father's death before he had a chance (ll. 63–70). Remember that it was an *elective* monarchy. Hamlet in his dying moments speaks in favour of Fortinbras becoming king (l. 350) and Horatio promises to convey his vote for this. So, Fortinbras who has 'some rights of memory in this kingdom' (l. 383) and who was given as the reason for the general unease at the beginning of the play, ends by becoming the strong and legitimate king, by whom order will be restored. The final, bloody conclusion can, when sensitively played, be moving, for in spite of the sudden death of four of the main characters Hamlet and Laertes are reconciled and justice of a rough kind has prevailed, though the ethics explored in the play (as we shall see) are not clear-cut. Notice how in his final speeches Hamlet seems thankful to be leaving 'this harsh world' and concerned only that Horatio should save him from a 'wounded name' in posterity—is this because of what has happened or is it perhaps consistent with his earlier disenchantment?

These exercises and commentary were designed to go some way towards answering the question 'what is the play about?', and the relative complexity of them illustrates that it is 'about' a number of things, all connected in a consistent manner and most of them treated fairly fully. It is this diversity, this richness, which makes the play so long and it is also one reason that it has proved an inexhaustible seam for critics to work.

What kind of interrelated subjects might I have in mind?

Those parts of *Hamlet* about the theatre and how they relate to the play's main action provide a good example. This is what Anne Barton calls the play's 'theatrical self-reference' (Introduction, p. 28), and among Shakespeare's plays *Hamlet* is 'unique in the density and pervasiveness' of references to plays and playing. You will perhaps recall how many examples Professor Gurr takes from it to illustrate his two cassette talks on the Elizabethan theatre (Cassette 1, sides A and B). Some of these references were very topical: Rosencrantz's account of the child actors, the 'little eyases' in II.2.338, referring to the War of the Theatres in 1601, requires as much explanation now as it would have required little at the time and is just contemporary satire. (There is a good account of this 'war' in the New Arden edition of the play.) Other allusions to plays and playing have a more general bearing and significance: Hamlet's advice to the plays and players in III.2 for example, or Polonius's catalogue of kinds of play at II.2.395 (*Hamlet*, incidentally, was the first play to be described as a 'Tragicall Historie' on the title page of the First and Second Quartos). In a broad sense, all these references are relevant to the main action because they explore and develop the notion of playing a part, which is precisely what Claudius, Hamlet and Gertrude are doing in the 'drama within a drama' taking place in the court at Elsinore (Claudius pretending grief at the late king's death, Hamlet with his 'antic disposition', etc.). One might also note, *en passant*, Shakespeare's continual interest in the *meaning* of theatre generally as a medium founded on enacted illusion. In a particular sense, certain references in the play are essential to the movement of the plot: Hamlet announces (II.2.602) 'The play's the thing/Wherein I'll catch the conscience of the King' and it is not until after Claudius's precipitate departure from 'The Mousetrap' that Hamlet fully accepts the ghost's account of his father's murder ('O good Horatio, I'll take the ghost's word for a thousand pound' III.2.295). Shortly after this, he kills Polonius in the belief that it is Claudius behind the arras (III.4).

Is there, though, an argument to be made *against* the value of some of the theatrical allusions?

I think that perhaps there is. Hamlet's advice to the players is memorable and revealing about the contemporary theatre and, by illustrating that he is a man interested in such matters, it is consistent with the main action but there seems to be a disproportionate amount of time spent on this—the same effects could perhaps have been produced with less elaboration. Similarly, the First Player's speech on Hecuba (II.2.466), although relevant to Hamlet's situation (see Introduction, set text page 30) as regards both its theme and its effect on him, is really rather lengthy. I am not necessarily suggesting that either of these scenes should be 'cut' (though they often have been) for they are part of the richness of the play. They are also a good example of the fullness of treatment which Shakespeare accords to almost all the subjects in the play. I think you will find this is so wherever you look, whether it is the characterization of Osric in Act V or the melancholy and suicide debated in Hamlet's soliloquies.

II.2 Hamlet (left) addresses Rosencrantz (centre) and Guildenstern

II.2 Rosencrantz (left) addresses Hamlet

IV.7 Claudius (right) and Laertes plot Hamlet's murder

But, to return to my first question (my introduction, p. 5), the play clearly isn't 'about' the theatre, or it is so only to a limited extent, though doubtless an ingenious and perverse critic could try to persuade you that that is its subject. Plays and playing, although enriching and enhancing, are an aspect only of the main action.

What *is* the main action?

The bare bones of the plot can be put in one sentence: the ghost of a murdered king appears to his son to urge him to take revenge which, after delays, he finally does in Act V in the course of which he, his mother and his own murderer die. The main reason that this seems a crudely inadequate, not to say misleading, account is that it fails to indicate the prominence of the character of the prince in the play—and it is a fairly safe bet that the name 'Hamlet' will evoke from 'China to Peru' the response 'To be or not to be . . .'. In other words, an outline of the plot alone is *Hamlet* without Hamlet.

Inescapably, anyone attempting to answer my first question finds himself or herself focussing on the subject of the second question, the character of Hamlet; and any discussion of the play, whether as 'revenge tragedy' or 'political drama' or whatever, has to take into account his absolute centrality in a way that is not the case with any one character in, for example, *Twelfth Night*. It is not that other characters in *Hamlet* are drawn in a perfunctory or superficial way, for even Osric, though a 'minor' figure, is very skilfully and economically drawn. It is, rather, that the character of Hamlet as Shakespeare drew him was truly something new, and the play in which he appears marked 'a cultural and historical watershed' (see set text Introduction, page 17).

V.2 Hamlet (left) with Horatio

V.2 Claudius brings Hamlet (left) and Laertes together

15

The character of *Hamlet* and the action of the play

NE aspect of the discussion of the character of Hamlet which must be mentioned lies in the nature of modern drama: there is the part and there is the actor, just as there is the reader and the text, and the two together form the character in the drama. Just as no two readers are the same, so every actor performs his own 'Hamlet'—if you look at the twenty-four illustrations on pages 26–7 you will get an idea of what celebrated versions there have been since the first production with Richard Burbage in the main part. (I say 'modern drama' in distinction from drama with more formalized methods of characterization such as the use of masks or allegorical figures or characters based on 'humours' or 'types'.)

In what follows, I shall refer to the character of Hamlet only as it may be described from the text in your edition of the play in an attempt to establish the nature and magnitude of Shakespeare's achievement in the portrayal of what is probably the most discussed character in Western literature. The imperative need to keep to the text, and the whole text, in discussing the characterization is readily illustrated by reading the performances of critics over the centuries. Patrick Cruttwell describes *the dangers of straying from the words Shakespeare wrote:

> . . . disagreements about Hamlet seem to have been of a special kind.
> They have involved a transference to ourselves, to within ourselves, of
> problems which should exist only inside the play, with the consequences
> of an all-befogging emotional subjectiveness.

A notorious example of this transference is Coleridge's remark 'I have a smack of Hamlet myself, if I may say so' (*Table Talk*, 24 June 1827). It expresses a feeling experienced by numerous readers whether positively, as with Keats's 'Hamlet's heart was full of such Misery as mine is' (*Letters*, August 1820(?)) or negatively, as with J. Alfred Prufrock's 'No! I am not Prince Hamlet, nor was meant to be' (T. S. Eliot's 'The Love Song of J. Alfred Prufrock'). Coleridge and Keats each took the aspect of the character of Hamlet which they felt they had themselves— for the former it was Hamlet's 'prevalence of the abstracting and generalizing habit over the practical', for the latter it was a depressed or despairing state of mind. In a similar way, each actor is likely to emphasize certain traits in the character, in spite of a director's view of the role.

Why is it that the character of Hamlet seems so readily to become a mirror to readers with a degree of imagination?

There are two reasons I can think of: he is a particularly 'modern' figure in Shakespearean drama, and he is (to many, at least) an *attractive* figure. His 'modernity' is part of Anne Barton's reason for describing the play as a' watershed':

> . . . the moment when 'modern' man—sceptical, complex, self-lacerating,
> uncertain of his relationships with other people and with a possible
> bogus world of heroic action—achieved artistic embodiment.

(Set text, p. 17)

It is not Hamlet alone who conveys the idea of this 'new' kind of man, for Horatio and Hamlet's fellow students Rosencrantz and Guildenstern contribute to it too.

---

* Cruttwell, P. (1963) 'The Morality of *Hamlet*—"Sweet Prince" or "Arrant Knave" ', *Stratford-Upon-Avon Studies*, vol. 5, Edward Arnold, p. 110.

But Hamlet is the most articulate character whose dilemmas force self-questioning on him and he is thus the main expression of such a man. Further, although he is made to question and reason in a manner appropriate to a seventeenth-century intellectual, he and his deliberations are not confined to that time in the way that, for example, Jimmy Porter, the 'angry young man' in John Osborne's play *Look Back in Anger*, is to the 1950s.

It is worth dwelling for a moment on the 'intellectual' aspect of the character, for Hamlet is unique among Shakespeare's creations in this respect. (Many another is given an impressive degree of perspicacity, self-analysis and articulateness but that is in part a convention of the dramatic mode and in part one aspect of Shakespeare's genius.) When we first meet Hamlet he has been asking consent for 'going back to school in Wittenberg' (I.2.113), that is, to return to the German University of Wittenberg founded in 1502, the favourite university of Danes studying abroad and made famous by its association with Martin Luther who nailed his theses to the door of the castle church there in 1517. The significance of Wittenberg is not especially that it was Protestant (for, in general, the atmosphere in *Hamlet* is redolent of catholicism) but that it had been 'reorganized on humanist principles' under the influence of Luther and Philip Melanchthon.* The use of the word 'humanist' has here to be understood in the Renaissance sense rather than the modern. Broadly speaking, it meant turning away from medieval scholasticism towards a more liberal attitude to learning, based on the study of Greek and Latin classical writing, though the Aristotelian emphasis on causation in scholastic thought remained much in evidence. You can see this in the soliloquies 'To be, or not to be' (III.1.56), 'How all occasions . . . ' (IV.4.32) and the speech 'What a piece of work' (II.2.303) where there is repeated emphasis on the role of reason in human existence. It was this which distinguished man from beast (remember, too, Hamlet's bitter comment on Gertrude's hasty re-marriage: 'O God, a beast that wants discourse of reason/Would have mourned longer'—I.2.150). The construction of the soliloquies is based on the process of reasoning and at every point in the plot Hamlet produces *reasons* for his actions or delays.

One of the subjects of the soliloquy 'To be, or not to be', suicide and death in general, is 'debated' in this way. The meditation on death (which is a continuous theme in the play) would not have seemed so prominent to an Elizabethan audience as it might to us, for it was a subject more openly discussed and dwelt upon than many think proper today. Suicide, for example, which is debated by Hamlet and then imputed to Ophelia, was the subject of a work by John Donne called *Biathanatos. A declaration of that paradoxe, or thesis, that Self-homicide is not so naturally Sinne, that it may never be otherwise.* This work, written 'probably in 1608' but not published in Donne's lifetime was, as John Carey has written,† 'Like Hamlet's "To be, or not to be", . . . a sign of the times. Men were starting to question the outright condemnation of suicide, which traditionalists had for centuries upheld'. Hamlet's beliefs are uncertain and to a degree agnostic. He appears to accept that 'the Everlasting' has 'fixed/His canon 'gainst self-slaughter' and, debating the matter in 'To be, or not to be', is uncertain about the afterlife, for it is 'the dread of something after death' (III.1.78) which is the real impediment to suicide. On the other hand the reason he gives for not killing Claudius in III.3.74 assumes that there *is* a Heaven. Yet Judgement, one of the Four Last Things in Christian eschatology, does not figure in his thinking about revenge. Another example of his cast of mind, and one suggestive of openness, is his celebrated remark 'There are more things in heaven and earth, Horatio,/Than are dreamt of in your philosophy (I.5.166; NB 'your' does not mean Horatio's specifically but 'philosophy generally', and the notion that a person has a 'philosophy' is in itself an intellectual one).

* Woodward, William H. (1906) *Studies in Education during the Age of the Renaissance: 1400–1600*, Cambridge University Press, p. 224; reprinted in Frye, R. M. (1963) *Shakespeare and Christian Doctrine*, Oxford, p. 71.
† Carey, John (1981) *John Donne, Life, Mind and Art*, Faber, p. 205.

To some extent, Hamlet is a figure representative of the time when the play was written in that his thinking embodies both doubt and belief, though the way each of these is expressed must be seen in relation to the events and action of the play. His agnosticism about the afterlife comes early in the play and, while perfectly consistent with his mood, could also perhaps be seen as expressing the kind of doubt probably felt by some of Shakespeare's audience for whom 'this world no longer, as in the medieval metaphor, mirrored the reality of the next'.* On the other hand, in the final scene of the play Hamlet expresses on two occasions a firm confidence in Providence (V.2.10 'There's a divinity that shapes our ends', and V.2.213: 'There is special providence in the fall of a sparrow';† the latter being a reference to Matthew 10:29) and this is dramatically appropriate. Taken together with the earlier soliloquies, these final affirmations also illustrate a degree of ambivalence characteristic of Renaissance thought. Good examples of this characteristic are to be found in the writing of men like Montaigne whose *Essais* were translated in 1603 by John Florio, or Peter de la Primaudaye whose *The French Academy* was published in 1594. No one knows for certain whether Shakespeare had read the latter, though it has a passage which is bound to call to mind Hamlet's speech 'What a piece of work is a man' (II.2.303 ff.):

> . . . When I admire the diversity of times and seasons, the continual spring of fountains, the certain course of rivers, and generally, so many wonderful works under the cope of heaven, I cannot marvel enough at the excellency of Man, for whom all these things were created and are maintained and preserved in their being and moving, by one and the same divine providence always like unto itself.

> (*Of Man*, I, i)

Hamlet's 'modern' sensibility and also his dilemma is perhaps particularly brought out in IV.4 where he reflects on the futility of Fortinbras's mission—yet, at the same time, as a prince himself he admires the spirit of the enterprise. What little we know of Fortinbras suggests that he suffers no such scruples or troubling thoughts.

It is in character that Hamlet should hold the drunken habits of the court under Claudius in contempt: 'We'll teach you to drink deep ere you depart' (I.2.175) he tells Horatio and later adds that 'This heavy-headed revel east and west/Makes us traduced and taxed of other nations' (I.4.17–18), and the way in which the criticism is made indicates that it is not the court itself which he is rejecting (as some critics have suggested). Indeed, he later refers to his own claim to the throne (V.2.65) and his references to 'honour' (IV.4.55–6) and his duty (I.5.189), his concern that posterity should know the truth (V.2.333) show him to be in concord with the standards of the ruling class he was born into. (Graham Martin takes a different view, as you will see in Block VI *King Lear*.) I am arguing, then, that he is a figure of his time and yet one not confined to it because he debates matters of timeless and universal interest in a recognizably 'modern' or open way—death, for example—and does not seem to come to firm or dogmatic conclusions.

I suggested earlier that Hamlet would also be to many people an attractive figure with whom it would be reasonable to identify. This may seem a curious suggestion in view of Hamlet's behaviour to Ophelia and his mother, not to mention the stabbing of Polonius and, if one takes L. C. Knights's view§ that Hamlet is a man 'who has given himself over to a false direction of consciousness', one is likely to disagree. The heart of the disagreement lies in one's view of the play's 'morality' (see my question 3, page 5) and I want to deal with this a little

---

* Elton, W. R. 'Shakespeare and the Thought of His Age' in Muir, K. and Schoenbaum, S. (eds.) (1971) *A New Companion to Shakespeare Studies*, Cambridge, p. 196.
† 'Special' here is actually a theological term referring to the care of God for individuals.
§ Knights, L. C. (1979) *Hamlet and Other Shakespearean Essays*, Cambridge University Press, p. 71.

later. For the present, let me again quote Patrick Cruttwell explaining the attractiveness of Hamlet:

> One of the odd things about Hamlet's character—and one of the things which makes it so often possible to compare him with a real person such as Donne—is that in practice we continually forget that *he is a prince.* Something seems to have almost obliterated that great difference between royalty and the rest which real life, at that time, certainly preserved and which is normally visible even in the Shakespearean drama itself. We do not have with Hamlet, as we do with Prince Hal, a deliberate 'stepping-down', and in fact we are never able to forget Prince Hal's rank, for he himself never forgets it. It is a matter with Hamlet of a relaxed informality of manner and an easy colloquialism of tone; they contrast very strongly, as I am sure they are meant to, with the formality of Claudius, the affectations of Osric, and the pomposity of Polonius. A great deal of Hamlet's attractiveness has always depended on this; all through the centuries readers and spectators alike have felt for him, as for no other character, I suspect, a delusion of equality and intimacy, and they have been all the more pleased with this delusion because they remembered, at moments, whom they were feeling it for. (We can be snobs in our imaginations just as much as in our lives.)
>
> (*op. cit.*, p. 127)

This seems to me a convincing argument which is well illustrated by Hamlet's dealings with the Players (III.1).

Where else do we see the more attractive side of Hamlet's personality?

There is his sense of humour which we see in his guying of Polonius (II.2) and, later, of Osric (V.2). He has, too, a friendly directness in his relationship with Horatio and, before he knows them to be spies, Rosencrantz and Guildenstern.

Another plausible explanation of Hamlet's appeal to men like Keats, Hazlitt and Goethe is his 'temperament'. His sense of humour notwithstanding, an Elizabethan audience would have had little difficulty in identifying him as 'melancholic', that is, one in whom there was, according to contemporary psychological explanations, a predominance of 'black bile'. (The other three 'humours' were 'blood', 'phlegm' and 'choler' which are the origins of our modern 'sanguine', 'phlegmatic', 'choleric', and we still talk of someone being in a 'good humour'. See also the Introduction page 35 to *Measure for Measure*.) It is important to remember that this was a way of describing a certain type of personality (as Jungian psychologists might talk of 'extroverts' and 'introverts') and it did not necessarily mean the same as the modern term 'depressed' although it could do. Timothy Bright, who wrote a *Treatise of Melancholy* published in 1586, describes some characteristics of 'melancholy men': they are sometimes 'very witty, and quickly discern', their melancholy 'breedeth a jealousy of doubt in that they take in deliberation, and causeth them to be the more exact and curious in pondering the very moments [i.e. 'causes'] of things . . . Their resolution riseth of long deliberation, because of doubt and mistrust which, as it is not easily bred, so it is also hard to remove . . . Their dreams are fearful . . . ' (chapter xxii, pages 129–31). You may recall from II.2 that Hamlet tells Rosencrantz 'I have bad dreams' (l. 254–5) and he evinces other symptoms listed by Bright—his comment that 'Denmark's a prison' (II.2.243) is one and his later assertion 'I am but mad north-north-west' (II.2.377) seems to accord with Bright's view that the best air for melancholics came from the south and south-east. It may be that these outward signs are assumed as part of his 'antic disposition' but they are, none the less, consistent with Hamlet's general disposition as Bright would have seen it and certainly Hamlet's capacity to ponder 'the very moments of things' is hardly open to question (and he might rightly be compared to Milton's *Il Penseroso* in this respect).

However, a more complex question (and one related to, but distinct from, temperament) is Hamlet's state of mind, what has occasioned it, and his 'madness'. When he first appears in the play, he is undoubtedly 'melancholy' in the sense of being 'depressed':

> . . . O God, God,
> How weary, stale, flat, and unprofitable
> Seem to me all the uses of this world!
>
> (I.2.132–3)

Further evidence, if any were needed, comes in I.4 when, warned by Horatio not to follow the ghost, he replies 'I do not set my life at a pin's fee' (l. 65); and later he tells Guildenstern 'I have of late—but wherefore I know not—lost all my mirth, forgone all custom of exercises . . . ' (II.2.295). This is a readily understandable frame of mind, given his situation, which Anne Barton sums up thus:

> Claudius has prevented Hamlet from succeeding to the throne of Denmark, contracted a scandalous marriage with Hamlet's mother, and accomplished both these things through the secret murder of the father Hamlet loved. By insisting that the Prince remain at court, rather than returning to university at Wittenberg, he forces him to confront these enormities daily.
>
> (*Set text*, p. 39)

Note how this account is based strictly on what we know from the text (although it is true we learn one of these facts near the end of the play, and one might add to the list Hamlet's anguish at his father's sufferings). It seems to me that this is the only satisfactory way to interpret Hamlet's subsequent delays and actions—in terms of what *happens* and what we are *told*. I now want to look at three aspects of the plot: (a) Hamlet's failure to kill Claudius, (b) his rejection of Ophelia, and (c) his denunciation of his mother's behaviour.

Hamlet and Claudius

THE principle riddle audience and critics alike have faced in discussing Hamlet is his behaviour towards Claudius. He twice berates himself for his failure to keep his promise to the ghost, most memorably in the soliloquy 'How all occasions . . . ' (IV.4.32), for by this time he is *sure* of Claudius's guilt. On the earlier occasion, 'O, what a rogue and peasant slave am I!' (II.2.547) he cannot be certain that the ghost is not a devil (l. 597). (Those of you familiar with *Macbeth* might remember how the witches are described as 'juggling fiends' that 'palter with us in a double sense'—V.7.19–20.) It is not until III.1 that even the audience knows for certain of Claudius's guilt by his own admission, prompted by 'The Mousetrap' in which Hamlet has indeed caught his 'conscience'—see II.2.603. If Hamlet is sure by III.3 that Claudius killed his father, why does he not act when he sees him at prayer and yet, in the very next scene, stabs Polonius believing him to be his 'better', that is, the king?

I suggest you spend a few moments thinking about how scenes III.3 and III.4 might actually be staged—what inferences one might draw from the *sequence* of events and what the implications are of the *exits* and *entrances*.

The crucial feature of the first of these scenes is surely that Hamlet makes his entrance *after* Claudius's soliloquy and his exit *before* the final couplet, the assumption being that he is not noticed by the king who is absorbed in his thoughts. The consequence of this is that he neither hears Claudius's admission of guilt nor does he learn of his impenitence and inability to pray (indicating that he is in a state of sin). In this lies the whole irony of the scene—according to the logic of his thoughts, stabbing Claudius would have been real revenge, for the latter would not have gone 'to heaven'. The reason that Hamlet gives for not taking action is hardly to his credit—that real revenge is not simply ending the life of his father's murderer but doing his best to ensure that he goes to eternal damnation. On the other hand, if you think carefully about the scene, it's possible to see another explanation. Could it be that Hamlet can't actually bring himself to stab a man apparently at prayer?

Look carefully at what Hamlet says from line 88 onwards, for it has a direct bearing on the next scene. How?

Simply that the next scene takes place in the Queen's closet (i.e. private quarters) so Hamlet assumes that a male voice is that of her husband, Claudius. While not in the 'pleasure of his bed', 'Claudius' (as Hamlet believes him to be) *is* in private with the Queen. More than that, he is *hidden* which could suggest to Hamlet that he is skulking like an illicit lover and also spying on him. By the time he stabs through the arras, he has been again reminded of his father's murder by the angry exchange at the beginning of the scene and so perhaps the necessary charge of feeling for the act has been generated. To stab his father's murderer in the presence of his mother but not actually in front of her could seem the perfect revenge but, as in the previous scene, an ironic twist robs his action of its purpose (and leads to a trail of consequences related to Polonius's children, Ophelia and Laertes).

I should mention some of the other, numerous explanations that have been offered for Hamlet's failure to act in the first of these two scenes and explain why I find them unconvincing. Most of them accept that squeamishness is not the reason, in spite of Hamlet's earlier conclusion that he must be 'pigeon-livered' (II.2.574) and he dispatches of Rosencrantz and Guildenstern briskly enough. One fairly common assumption is that Hamlet is suffering from a neurotic failure of the will to act. The extreme version of this interpretation is the Freudian psychoanalytical explanation, based on the theory of the 'Oedipus complex', that

> The call of duty to kill his stepfather cannot be obeyed because it links itself with the unconscious call of his nature to kill his mother's husband, whether this is the first or the second; the absolute 'repression' of the former impulse involves the inner prohibition of the latter also.
>
> (Ernest Jones, *Hamlet and Oedipus*, Gollancz, 1949)

Given Hamlet's reiterated disgust at the sexuality of women and his remarks to his mother (which a Freudian critic might see as indicative of an unconscious and repressed incestuous desire), it is fairly easy to see how this approach might be developed and L. C. Knights (whose view of the play I cited earlier) thinks that 'there is enough . . . to give plausibility to the psycho-analytical speculations of Dr Ernest Jones' (*op. cit.* p. 54). He regards what he calls Hamlet's 'paralysis' as the result of 'health giving way to disease' (p. 70). I don't find this a convincing interpretation, mainly because I don't think Shakespeare means Hamlet's character to be seen entirely in neurotic terms. He *is* depressed, though it is hardly true to say, as T. S. Eliot did, that his 'emotion . . . is in excess of the facts as they appear'*—surely he has many reasons for feeling sick of life? But the main objection to a psychoanalytical interpretation has to be that it is treating the character of Hamlet as a 'real' person and not sticking simply to what we observe and are told.

In the introduction to the set text, another explanation of the two scenes is offered (p. 41) based on the belief that Hamlet can't really bring himself to murder a man face to face and that, in any case, he sees the futility of revenge. Well put though they are, I am not convinced by either of these points because the first is inconsistent with what Hamlet actually tells us in the scene—that he wants him not only to die but also to go to hell—and the second is inconsistent with what follows (look at the exchange between Hamlet and the ghost later in III.4 and then at the soliloquy in IV.4). A more interesting question is why Hamlet continues to fail to act. The soliloquy in IV.4 shows Hamlet asking himself this.

What conclusions does he come to and what is the point of Fortinbras and his army being in the scene?

To take the second question first, the principal reason for Fortinbras being in the scene is to set up a contrast between his 'honourable' activity in a pointless cause and Hamlet's failure to perform a duty. (There is also the secondary reason that the qualities displayed in this venture are one of the factors which makes him a suitable candidate for office as king in V.2.) As for Hamlet, what we learn from the soliloquy is that he doesn't know why he still has not exacted his revenge. Though he cannot give an explanation, it's possible to infer his state of mind and thus a reason from the emphases within the speech. Notice how anger and desire for revenge (which he admits is now 'dull') seem to have evaporated, to be replaced by guilt at inaction and a *reasoned* realization of a princely duty to 'honour'. As Brian Stone points out in his contribution to the Forum, there is a gradual progression in Hamlet's thinking through the play. One can persuasively argue that it is the closet scene which has lanced the boil of his anger and that in IV.4 he is motivated more by duty than hatred, though the duty is not (as I have indicated earlier) without its attendant dilemmas for him. To see Hamlet's thinking in IV.4 in terms of duty is to raise the question of ethics and the play's morality and you might spend a few moments thinking about the extent to which these are considered and whether a consistent pattern emerges, for I shall be considering them a little later. So far I have argued that Hamlet's behaviour towards Claudius and his thinking can be reasonably explained, but what of his treatment of Ophelia? Is he truly mad?

* Eliot, T. S. (1963) 'Hamlet' in *Selected Prose*, Penguin Books, p. 102.

Hamlet and Ophelia

THE crucial episode between Hamlet and Ophelia is the so-called 'nunnery scene' (III.1) and I suggest you turn back to your answers to the questions I posed in the earlier exercises, especially as to how the scene should be directed. Think, too, about Hamlet's statements about his 'madness' in I.5 and V.2.

The first we hear of Hamlet's strange behaviour is Ophelia's report to Polonius in II.2 which follows immediately on his warning to Horatio in the previous scene:

> How strange or odd some'er I bear myself—
> As I perchance hereafter shall think meet
> To put an antic disposition on—
>
> (I.5.170–3)

Given its context, this apparently sudden decision can only be seen as a tactic to cover the revenge he has just promised to the ghost and in V.2 this is the justification he offers Laertes for having killed Polonius. The scene Ophelia describes (II.1) would, if it were played, be both alarming and *comic*, though she doesn't find it so. We have to remember that for the Elizabethan audience lunacy was considered comic (think of Malvolio in *Twelfth Night*) and the account of Hamlet's appearance and mad stares would have provoked amusement even if it fails to do so today when insanity isn't considered funny. Similarly, Hamlet's guying of Polonius introduces another form of humour combining 'wit' and lunacy. (The significance of his having 'No hat upon his head' is that in Elizabethan times

The 'nunnery' scene from the RSC production of Hamlet *in 1961 (Photo: Holte Photos Ltd)*

most people wore hats indoors.) This encounter is only described but in III.1 the two meet face to face after the soliloquy 'To be, or not to be'. Clearly Ophelia thinks Hamlet is still mad ('O, what a noble mind is here o'erthrown!' l. 151), so presumably he is still feigning a lunatic manner (though this is seldom if ever done in modern productions). Remember, though, that he is being watched by Claudius who comes to a different conclusion:

> Nor what he spake, though it lacked form a little,
> Was not like madness . . .

> (l. 164–5)

There is then a disjunction between the way he behaves and what he actually says, for, although Ophelia cannot understand the reasons for his harsh rejection of her, his words make consistent sense, apart from the apparent contradiction of 'I did love you once' and 'I loved you not'. I think we are meant to believe that Hamlet *did* once love Ophelia (there is her word and the letters as testimony) but that over the months since his father's death and mother's re-marriage his state of feelings, towards her and everybody, has changed (as he has told Rosencrantz and Guildenstern in the previous scene). His feelings towards women in particular have changed because of the outrage occasioned by his mother's re-marriage so that Ophelia has to bear the brunt of his revulsion at his mother's behaviour and consequent fury with the deception of women in general (l. 143). We have to remember that the action takes place over a number of months and that Ophelia has, in a sense, made it easier for him by her reported coyness in rejecting his letters as her father commanded. It could well be argued that the assertion 'I loved you not' is in fact a kind lie, for to say you have fallen out of love with someone is surely more hurtful than saying you never loved them? The scene is undoubtedly a shocking one and it is meant to be so—just as the 'closet scene', which I shall come to in the next section, is—but then, as Horatio is later to say, it is a play about 'carnal, bloody and unnatural acts'. In case you should think I am using too much imagination in my interpretation of this scene, I would ask you to note, as I pointed out in 'Commentary and Exercises', that we are forced to our own explanation as we are not actually told of Hamlet's specific feelings and that I have argued only from what can actually be found *in the text* and from how it might be staged.

Hamlet and his mother

HE confrontation between Hamlet and Gertrude in III.4 is probably the most shocking scene of the play for several reasons.

If you agree, what would you say these are?

The situation as it develops, with the *reversal* of the usual role of mother upbraiding child, touches some instinctive nerve in most audiences, especially as the scene begins with Gertrude's spirited if hopelessly optimistic attempt to exert her parental role. Look at Hamlet's reply to her question 'Have you forgot me?' (i.e. 'Who I am—your mother'):

> No, by the Rood, not so!
> You are the Queen, your husband's brother's wife,
> And, would it were not so, you are my mother.
>
> (III.4.15–17)

Not only is this very strong language, for as 'Rood' means 'Cross of Christ', Hamlet is virtually saying 'By Christ', it is also a very specific indictment of her wrong doing—committing incest. When Hamlet earlier used the term 'incestuous sheets' (I.2.157), the force of the adjective is likely to slip by a modern audience. According to church teaching in England at the time, incest included a woman's marrying her husband's brother (based on Leviticus, 20:21), and Hamlet's first bitter aside 'A little more than kin, and less than kind!' (I.2.65) in response to being called 'my son' by Claudius would have had a particular resonance for an Elizabethan audience. The incestuous nature of the union is repeated by the ghost: 'that incestuous, that adulterate beast' (referring to Claudius, I.5.42) and 'damned incest' (I.5.83); and also by Hamlet in III.3, 'th'incestuous pleasure of his bed' (l. 90); and finally at the end as he forces Claudius to drink the poisoned cup (V.2.319). It is this union and its implications which is really what is 'rotten in the state of Denmark' and responsible for the atmosphere of unease which prevails at the beginning of the play where Horatio interprets the ghost's appearance as boding 'some strange eruption to our state' (I.1.69). What he has in mind is the civil disturbance caused by Fortinbras but the word equally applies to the situation at court.

'Eruption' is particularly appropriate in this context for it suggests a boil or a pustule and it is this kind of imagery which is continually employed throughout the play to describe sexual relationships. Human sexuality figures centrally in the next play you study, *Measure for Measure*, and it is a prominent theme in *Hamlet* but not so much for the frequency with which it is discussed as for the virulent emotions, the destructive passions aroused by it. Practically all the sexual references in *Hamlet* are in terms of putrefaction and disease: in I.3 Laertes warns Ophelia to be on her guard against 'contagious blastments' (l. 42) and the 'canker' (l. 39) and this is followed by Hamlet's corresponding references to 'good kissing carrion' (II.2.182) and then his lewd exchanges with Ophelia 'Do you think I mean country matters' (III.2.125), though these are part of the 'antic disposition'. The most blistering expressions come in his denunciation of his mother which is packed with disgust and abhorrence for sexual love:

> In the rank sweat of an enseamèd bed,
> Stewed in corruption, honeying and making love
> Over the nasty sty—
>
> (III.4.93–5)

'In England,' lamented Max Beerbohm in 1889, 'Hamlet has

long ceased to be treated as a play. It has become simply a hoop

through which every eminent actor must, sooner or later, jump.'

1
2
3
4
5
6

7
8
9
10
11
12

13
14
15
16
17
18

19
20
21
22
23
24

1 **Richard Burbage** (*c. 1567–1619*). The creator, date unknown. In July 1602 the play was said to have been 'latelie Acted by the Lord Chamberleyne his servants'. Burbage's funeral elegy mentions Hamlet as one of his most popular roles.

2 **Thomas Betterton** (*c. 1635–1710*). From 1661 (Lincoln's Inn Fields) to 1709, when over 70, he acted 'a young man of great expectation, vivacity, and enterprise'.

3 **David Garrick** (*1717–1779*). Drury Lane, 1742. Played every season until retirement, 1776. Magnificent with Ghost: 'Shudder after shudder ran through one before he began to speak' (Lichtenberg); Fielding made much of this point in *Tom Jones*.

4 **John Philip Kemble** (*1757–1823*). Drury Lane, 1783. Gloomiest of Hamlets in the theatre of the Romantic movement, he was intensely introspective. Superb aspect. Wore modern Court dress of rich black velvet; hair in powder.

5 **William Henry West Betty** (*1791–1874*). Master Betty, the Young Roscius. House of Commons adjourned to see the boy (Drury Lane, 1805). Handsome, precocious, with a sponge-like memory. His fame was transient; died forgotten.

6 **Edmund Kean** (*1787–1833*). Drury Lane, 1814. Less consistent than Kemble, his Hamlet was a sequence of strong dramatic moments, varying between the electrifying and the exaggerated.

7 **William Charles Macready** (*1793–1873*). Covent Garden, 1821. An intellectual, eloquent Hamlet with a subtlety that in later years would become excessive.

8 **Henry Irving** (*1838–1905*). Lyceum, 1874. The scholar's Hamlet: flexible, poetic, deeply affectionate. Irving could excite in his intense, charged quietness as much as in passion.

9 **Johnstone Forbes-Robertson** (*1853–1937*). Lyceum, 1897. Always the 'sweet prince', he spoke with unfailing nobility. 'The true classical Hamlet' (Shaw). His production restored Fortinbras – long omitted – to the stage.

10 **Herbert Beerbohm Tree** (*1853–1917*). Haymarket, 1892. Romantic, erratic, sentimental. His resolutely elaborate production ended upon 'Flights of angels sing thee to thy rest', with chorus.

11 **Sara Bernhardt** (*1844–1923*). Paris, 1899, in French prose version; London (Adelphi) and Stratford, same year. A practical, courageous Hamlet. For Max Beerbohm '*tres grande dame*'.

12 **John Barrymore** (*1882–1942*). New York, 1922; Haymarket, London, 1925. American actor's performance, slow, firmly reasonable, without much sense of language. 'All that intellect could do was done' (Agate).

13 **John Gielgud** (*born 1904*). Old Vic and Queen's, spring, 1930, and many times subsequently. Definitive Hamlet of his generation, a youth desperately frustrated and disillusioned. Vocally, a Stradivarius controlled by a master.

14 **Laurence Olivier** (*born 1907*). Old Vic, 1937; Elsinore that summer. Less the Hamlet of indecision than the flash and outbreak of a fiery mind. 'Master of riposte, with tongue as with sword' (Ivor Brown). Film, 1948.

15 **Alec Guinness** (*born 1914*). Old Vic, 1938: modern-dress production; atmosphere of Ruritanian levee, gentle and moving; qualities that 1951 performance (New; traditional dress) lacked.

16 **Paul Scofield** (*born 1922*). Stratford, 1948: alternated with Robert Helpmann in Victorian setting; romantic, haunted Hamlet of great pathos. Moscow, London, 1955: notable Peter Brook production.

17 **Michael Redgrave** (*born 1908*). New (for Old Vic), 1950: 'a less lyrical, less ethereal, more agonised, more actual Hamlet than most' (Ivor Brown). Stratford, 1958: commanding in mien and speech, and charting the soliloquies minutely.

18 **Richard Burton** (*born 1925*). Old Vic, 1953: solid, painstaking performance. John Neville (Fortinbras) was Hamlet – more touching and responsive – during the autumn of 1957. Burton acted the part (modern dress), New York, 1964; Gielgud production.

19 **Ian Bannen** (*born 1928*). Stratford, 1961. A neurotic, feverish youth. An odd caprice; sat in the players' property-trunk (the lid would fall on him) for the 'rogue and peasant slave' soliloquy.

20 **Peter O'Toole** (*born 1934*). National Theatre opening 1963. A tormented spirit who did not always communicate his torment. A recognizable portrait in its harsh way, but without much warmth.

21 **Innokenty Smoktunovsky** (*born 1925*). Russian film, 1964, much acclaimed in Britain. 'A smouldering blond brooder who leads the field [of film Hamlets]' (Kenneth Tynan). Director: Grigori Kozintsev.

22 **Christopher Plummer** (*born 1929*). BBC 1964 television production for the 400th anniversary of Shakespeare's birth. 'A romantic who learns to face realities' (*The Times*). Filmed at Elsinore. Ghost scene on beach to sound of roaring waves.

23 **David Warner** (*born 1941*). Stratford and London, 1965/6. Tortured young man, on brink of maturity, disillusioned, reaching a terrible fatalism. 'Warner's performance got more of humanity into the part than any previous Hamlet I've seen' (Ronald Bryden).

24 **Nicol Williamson** (*born 1938*). Round House (London) and America, 1969. Had authority and technique. Did not recognize the 'sweet prince'. This was a splenetic Hamlet, rasping in tone, harsh in demeanour. Film 1970.

27

Such descriptions of love-making are shocking enough in themselves but for a son to be using them to describe his mother's sexual relationship with her husband is doubly so, for it breaks a common taboo—the fiction children employ that their parents are asexual. Hamlet has already touched on this in his sneering remark:

> You cannot call it love. For at your age
> The heyday in the blood is tame

(III.4.69–70)

That is, 'at your age, you're past it'—or should be, is perhaps the implication.

If we are right to see this as the turning point in the action of the play, one of the reasons (apart from the change henceforth in Hamlet's feelings) is that Gertrude accepts the condemnation and her guilt (as Claudius already has done)—see IV.5.17. This is important because it confirms that, unlike a similar outburst by King Leontes in *The Winter's Tale*, Hamlet's disgust is based on something which has *actually taken place* in the play.

I used this expression deliberately because by now it is probably clear how I would answer the question posed on page 5 'is it legitimate to discuss the character of Hamlet independently of the dramatic action?' Think about this for a moment before going on.

It is certainly possible to do so, as numerous instances testify and, after all, no one can actually legislate as to how a person discusses a play. None the less, a number of 'problems' which have always been associated with the play are considerably diminished and in some instances removed by paying close attention to what we are actually told in the text and by discussing all the characters in the context of the action of which they are a part. Harold Jenkins, the editor of the Arden edition of the play, describes this approach and compares it with the 'character-centred' view:*

> By the end of the nineteenth century, the great age of character
> criticism as of the novel, it was possible to read, in a work significantly
> published in the year of Bradley's *Shakespearean Tragedy*, that Hamlet
> 'is in relation to its motive and main interest, a purely psychological
> study, and to that study the whole action of the drama is subordinated'.
> It is no less possible however, to see the matter in reverse, with the
> 'action of the drama' pre-eminent in shaping a significant design while
> the 'psychological' interest of the characters' motivation has a subsidiary
> importance in giving the action plausibility.

I am not arguing that *Hamlet* is a play without some difficulties (and the greatest of these concerns its morality which I have yet to discuss) but that some of them have been unnecessarily exaggerated. Further, I am sure that Anne Barton is correct when she comments, and not as a criticism, that 'at the heart of *Hamlet* lie a number of riddling and important silences' (Introduction, p. 37) and the effect of some of these, as is the case with Hamlet's delay, is that 'the audience is forced to draw conclusions—necessarily tentative—from his speech and behaviour, as though he were not a dramatic character but someone known in real life' (p. 40). And so we have yet another reason for the 'character' approach to the play.

* Jenkins, Harold (ed.) (1982) *Hamlet*, the Arden Edition of the Works of William Shakespeare, Methuen, p. 124.

Tragedy, Revenge Tragedy, and the ethics of vengeance

ET me now go back to that other question, 'what is the play about?' and its corollary 'what kind of play is it?' Is it, I asked, 'the tragedy of an individual' or is it 'a political and historical drama'?

I have frequently referred to the 'main action' and discussed the character of Hamlet in relation to this, and my own view is probably fairly clear by now from the discussion and commentary. It seems to me a remarkably rich and consistent play which leads me to say that it is both the tragedy of an individual *and* a political and historical drama, for, as is often the case in Shakespeare's work, private and public destinies, the fate of the individual and that of the state are intertwined and indivisible. It is interesting to note that, *pace* Polonius's catalogue in II.2, the play was actually designated in the First (1603) Quarto as 'The Tragicall Historie of Hamlet, Prince of Denmark by William Shake-speare' although in the First Folio (1623) it becomes simply 'The Tragedie of Hamlet, Prince of Denmarke'. The important part of the title is clearly 'tragedie', and 'historie' is used to mean 'account', for the distinction between 'history' and 'story' did not develop until later. Some discussion of 'Shakespearean Tragedy' (including a consideration of my earlier question (4) on *Antony and Cleopatra*, page 5) will follow in Block VI *King Lear* so let it suffice to point out here just two characteristics which an Elizabethan audience would have expected from a 'tragedy'. The first of these was the social position of the main characters:

> When Shakespeare's literate contemporaries went to see a tragedy, they confidently expected it to deal with people of high estate, not with the middle or lower classes of society. Tragedy had been for so long so closely associated with the 'fall of princes' theme . . . that Elizabethans could scarcely have conceived of the kind of tragedy of the common man which Mr Arther Miller attempts to create in our own time.*

The second characteristic was the inevitable fate of the main characters, and perhaps you remember the explanation in *A Midsummer Night's Dream* as to why 'Pyramus and Thisby' is a tragedy:

> And tragical, my noble lord, it is;
> For Pyramus therein doth kill himself.

> (V.1.66–7)

Frye, commenting on this, explains that

> This particular conception of tragedy, like the others suggested in Shakespeare, can in no sense cover all that Shakespeare actually achieved, but the cumulative effect of these references is to illustrate an Elizabethan conception of tragic themes which went little beyond the violence of melodrama.

> (*op. cit.* p. 103)

A sophisticated Aristotelian conception of tragedy was certainly not in the minds of Shakespeare and his audience, however much it came to dominate the thinking of later critics; and it has been suggested to me that one of the reasons for the original success of the play might have been the appeal of the violence of the final scene and a pleasure in the fall of members of the wicked, ruling élite. As I pointed out at the beginning of this block, *Hamlet* would certainly have been recognized

* Frye, Roland Mushat (1982) *Shakespeare. The Art of the Dramatist*, Allen & Unwin, pp. 101–2.

as belonging to the specific category of 'revenge tragedy' with all the expectations that that would have aroused. Furthermore, an Elizabethan audience would have been well aware of the Biblical text 'Vengeance is mine, I will repay, saith the Lord' and the prohibition of private revenge by the Christian Churches, but their feelings would have been mixed for, as Helen Gardner explains,* 'the essence of any tragedy of revenge is that its hero has not created the situation in which he finds himself and out of which the tragedy arises'. In Hamlet's situation, the avenging of his father is put to him as a duty and the curious feature of the play is that the morality of the action is never questioned as it is in other works in the genre (in Chapman's *Bussy D'Ambois*, for instance, a distinction is drawn by one character between 'murtherous minds' and 'just revengers'). Usually, the hero, though the innocent party, had to kill, so that the 'moral feelings of the audience are confused between satisfaction and outrage' (Helen Gardner, *op. cit.*). In fact it was common for the feelings of the audience towards the revenger to undergo a change in the course of the action from initial sympathy for his predicament to condemnation for his actions.

How does Hamlet fare in this respect?

By the final lines of the play a number of developments have taken place with extraordinary rapidity. Hamlet, relatively tranquil at the beginning of the scene, has sought forgiveness of Laertes who in turn is to ask it of him. In spite of having dispatched Polonius, Rosencrantz, Guildenstern and finally Claudius, Hamlet appears to die without losing his honour or the sympathy of the audience. We can say this because of Horatio's farewell to him ('Now cracks a noble heart . . .' V.2.353) and because of Fortinbras's act of homage, and one of the reasons must be that he is himself finally the victim, killed by treachery when he himself has used none. In a strange way, he is referred to almost as a martyr whose death has been incurred in an action, the result of which is the restoration of the kingdom to strong, legitimate rule. The attention is focussed on Hamlet and Horatio and not on the deaths of the other characters, partly because they happen so rapidly and have seemed inevitable to the conclusion of the plot.

Is there, in fact, a 'moral problem' posed by the action of the play?

In the sense that Shakespeare never raises the question, the answer has to be 'no', yet it must occur to any watcher that there is something of a contradiction between the Christian context and what seems to be condoned. It is, for example, strange that the ghost who announces that he is in Purgatory (I.5.11) should incite Hamlet to vengeance. The prevailing consciousness is that of Catholic Christianity with several references to the sacraments (Confession, Communion, the Last Rites: I.5.77, V.2.46) and the charge of incest is based on the church's teaching about kinship, yet the action of the play illustrates the very opposite of compassion and 'turning the other cheek'. The play doesn't therefore seem altogether consistent from a theological point of view, but then it is not a play about theology or (at least in the strict sense) a didactic work. Some critics have seen the play as being 'confused' but it could be argued that in its very inconsistencies it could be said to 'hold, as 'twere, the mirror up to nature, to show her own feature, scorn her own image, and the very age and body of the time his form and pressure' (III.2.21 ff.), though the obvious reply to this defence is that 'art isn't life'.

My own feeling is that Shakespeare wasn't especially interested in the moral questions implicit in the action—they simply don't feature in the way that they do in, for example, *Measure for Measure*. Others have seen the ending of the play as designed to make a more definite, critical point about the revenge ethic—Anne

---

* Gardner, Helen (1959) 'The Historical Approach to *Hamlet*' in *The Business of Criticism*, OUP.

Barton argues that in *Hamlet* Shakespeare has created a character who is 'too intelligent to be able to deceive himself into Laertes's belief that revenge can constitute . . . a meaningful redress of the situation' and who thus 'exposes the fundamental futility of the revenge code' (Introduction, p. 41). If this is so, it's difficult to see why he decides to take Claudius with him in the final moments of his life. What *does* interest Shakespeare in the ending, it seems to me, is that Hamlet dies with 'honour' and that order is restored to Denmark. Consequently, I have also to disagree with the view that 'the ending of *Hamlet* resolves nothing that really matters' (p. 51) because it seems to me that the 'public/political' aspect of the action is important within the play, even if the wider, more personal and metaphysical questions raised (in the soliloquies particularly) have proved more interesting to generations of commentators. Some critics (including Graham Martin, as you'll see in his contribution to the Forum) think that Shakespeare failed artistically to get these two aspects balanced or integrated. As you probably realize, it's not my own view, though I don't think the play is without its weaknesses—the moral contradiction I've mentioned being one, an *embarras de richesses* being another.

I would like to conclude by returning for a moment to the question of 'convention' and reminding you of Nick Furbank's remark (Block I, p. 31) that, paradoxically, to us, it is the way Shakespeare uses conventions that makes him *original*. It is perhaps salutary to remind ourselves that 'originality' did not have the modern sense of 'invention from nothing' until the eighteenth century and it was not, in our sense, a quality especially valued. In Block I, Nick Furbank makes the interesting point that Shakespeare's audience, familiar with an earlier play on the story of the Danish prince, would be expecting him to be *truly* mad (which, as I pointed out earlier, was often the case in 'revenge tragedy') and also that he would achieve vengeance in the course of the play rather than at its very end. He argues that the fact that Hamlet is only feigning lunacy (although he is, in the clinical sense, suffering a neurosis), and the delay in killing Claudius (with all Hamlet's doubts and self-questioning) compel the audience to '*re-evaluate* conventional categories and received ideas'. This is not to say, as Anne Barton does, that such ideas are being exposed as completely futile but that they are examined and questioned and that Shakespeare's originality resides in 'playing upon popular expectations but continually baffling and transcending them' (Block I, p. 31).

Hamlet—a 'revenge tragedy'? A study of 'melancholy'? A 'Christian' play? These questions bring us full circle to the beginning of this study and by now you are probably well on the way to forming a view of your own of the play. You will have an opportunity to look at some of the major speeches in the play again in the next section, 'The Language of the Play', which is followed by a 'Forum' of views from other members of the course team, and then a short selection of extracts from critics and commentators from Shakespeare's time to our own.

RD

 *The Language of the Play*

In these exercises I want to look at the different levels on which language can operate in a play. On one level it provides basic information about what happens in terms of event and character. As we experience the drama, however, we can notice other, subtle ways language is operating, telling us about event or character more indirectly. We, as audience or reader, are privy to these other levels in a way the characters are not, because we can see the self-conscious art of the dramatist at work: we are not simply involved emotionally in a dramatic experience, but can also 'see around' the immediate dramatic moment and make connections of meaning from a position outside the drama itself.

We can observe such different levels of language at work in Claudius's first speech to the Danish court (I.2). It contains necessary factual information about events which we need to register plus the intended message Claudius wishes to get across to his courtiers. But there are also other levels of meaning about Claudius observable through Shakespeare's art, through the form and structuring of this speech; from these we learn things about the dramatic situation and about Claudius himself which are not part of *his* experience. At these levels of meaning we enjoy a certain distance from the play, a consciousness of our relation to the play as audience rather than as vicarious members of the Danish court or Hamlet's friends. As audience we pick up and carry with us the possibilities and potential problems of meaning we expect the rest of the drama, literally, to act out. Many of the potentialities which impel our interest forward arise from the different levels of meaning we find operating in the language of the play.

We can begin looking at the various ways language operates by examining Claudius's first speech, I.2.1–39. You may remember Graham Martin's discussion of it in the section on Shakespeare's language in the Course Guide. Notice how the speech falls into two quite distinct sections at line 16.

What do you consider to be the intended information in this speech? And what is the indirect information we receive about Claudius? In other words, how does Shakespeare suggest things about Claudius of which he himself is unaware?

In the first sixteen lines we are informed that Claudius has married Gertrude despite the recent death of his brother, who was Gertrude's husband and the King of Denmark. The intention of Claudius's speech is to express his thanks to his courtiers for agreeing to his action. In lines 17–39 Claudius reports events we already know about from Horatio's account in I.1, that Fortinbras is taking advantage of uncommon circumstances to insist upon the return of lands legally lost by his father in combat with the former King Hamlet. To put a stop to this, Claudius is sending ambassadors to Fortinbras's uncle, urging him to curb his nephew's activities.

How, on another level, do we identify the information in this speech which is unintended by the speaker, but intended by Shakespeare? The actual words Claudius uses are chosen very carefully, since his character and situation demand that he appear confident of his position and power: he did not get where he is without the ability to manipulate, to select the appropriate words to justify his desires. It is this manipulation which Claudius would not intend the court to notice, but which we can observe in the syntax and structure of his speech, which subtly reveals the most questionable aspects of Claudius's position while overtly expressing his assuredness.

Compare the difference in syntax and sentence construction in the first section (lines 1–16) and the second section (lines 17–39). Start by simply identifying the clauses in lines 1–14 in which Claudius—the royal 'we'—is the subject, and make a note of anything which strikes you about their location. Then compare these features of sentence structure with the most obvious features of lines 17–39.

Don't be surprised, or dismayed, if you found it difficult to locate these clauses in the first two sentences. It seems to me they are purposefully hidden. I located the first one in lines 6–7 and the second one spread out from lines 8–14!

Though yet of Hamlet our dear brother's death
The memory be green, and that it us befitted
To bear our hearts in grief, and our whole kingdom
To be contracted in one brow of woe,   4

> Yet so far hath discretion fought with nature
> That *we* with wisest sorrow *think on him*
> Together *with remembrance of ourselves.*
> Therefore *our* sometime *sister*, now our Queen,   8
> Th' imperial jointress of this warlike state,
> *Have we*, as 'twere with a defeated joy,
> With an auspicious and a dropping eye,
> With mirth in funeral and with dirge in marriage,   12
> In equal scale weighing delight and dole,
> *Taken to wife.*

When looked at in isolation from the qualifying clauses that surround them, these two clauses express the least palatable ideas in Claudius's speech: his own self-interest in the brief mourning for his brother and his incestuous marriage with his brother's widow. It is not surprising, therefore, that these are the ideas which are most hidden by qualifying clauses which act to soften or disguise their unadorned reality. In contrast to this section, the complications of syntax in the second section emphasize and colour the Fortinbras intrigue to display where Claudius feels more confident of support. His sense of ability to control the situation is provided by long, elaborate explanations supported by strong but brief declarations and commands:

lines 17	Now follow that you know
25	So much for him
26	Now for ourself and for this time of meeting
27	Thus much the business is
27–8	. . . we have here writ/To Norway
33–4	. . . And we here dispatch/You . . .
39	Farewell; and let your haste commend your duty

The contrast in the structuring of the two sections of Claudius's speech reveals the differences in their content. The less savoury and more dangerous aspect of Claudius is camouflaged by the business over Fortinbras, where he can become clearly assertive, feeling himself to be on safe ground.

The subtle levels of meaning we have looked at with reference to Claudius are not confined to him or to passages of dialogue or public speech. Hamlet's soliloquies, although ostensibly direct expressions of Hamlet's view of himself and his situation are also sources of questions and problems which crucially affect both our understanding of Hamlet, the character, and the play as a whole.

Look now at Hamlet's first soliloquy (I.2.129–39). What new factual information does it contain? What is the main information about Hamlet conveyed by this speech?

The single fact we learn is the actual length of time which has elapsed—scarcely two months—since the death of King Hamlet, and that it is only one month since Hamlet's mother's marriage to his uncle. The extensive and important information communicated here, however, is concerned with feeling rather than fact. Even then we are informed about different levels of feeling. The essence of this soliloquy, which comes through in the comparisons Hamlet makes between his uncle and his father and in his description of his mother, is his sense of revulsion at the precipitate marriage of mother with uncle. Hamlet's soliloquy posits and develops a contrast between himself on the one hand, and his mother, father and uncle on the other, and one way he effects this contrast is through his choice of verbs. There is, for example, a marked frequency of verbs of action in Hamlet's description of his parent's marriage and his mother's and uncle's relationship: 'grown', 'fed', 'followed', 'married', 'post'; these are supported by phrases which further emphasize movement and action: 'increase of appetite', 'wicked speed', 'such dexterity'.

If you compare these lines with those which open the soliloquy, how does the general effect of the contrast inform us about Hamlet and his relation to his family and the court?

It seems to stress Hamlet's position as essentially that of an observer of all this activity. His energy and activity here are centred exclusively in his feelings, and their intensity is expressed almost despite himself in parenthetical expressions suggesting that words are almost beyond him: 'O God, God', 'Fie on't, ah, Fie', or else they explicitly express his aversion to the pain of putting such intense feelings into words: 'Heaven and earth, /Must I remember', 'Let me not think on't'. The impact of the soliloquy's opening statement, moreover, relies on Hamlet's desire to escape from all active thought and feeling, by passively disappearing:

> O that this too too sullied flesh would melt,
> Thaw, and resolve itself into a dew. (I.2.129–8)

(Note that these two lines form a famous crux in *Hamlet* scholarship, as Harold Brooks points out in Cassette 3, side B.)

How would you analyse the role of the last two lines of the soliloquy?

> It is not, nor it cannot come to good.
> But break, my heart, for I must hold my tongue.

In one sense they summarize Hamlet's whole feeling, extending it outward in time and space: 'It *is* not, nor it *cannot* come to good'; the present and future as well as the personal and public come together in that simple statement. We are directed to consider the relevance of Hamlet's personal grief to general conditions in the Danish court. Then, momentarily, we turn back again to Hamlet's own feeling ('But break my heart'), only to be redirected to the general implications arising from those feelings: 'For I must hold my tongue'. The movement in the brief sequence of statements affects the movement of our attention and thought, making us actively consider why Hamlet should say this. We are left holding the ball, wondering about the reasons for Hamlet's conclusion, ready to attend further to subsequent information that might answer these half-formulated questions. The soliloquy ends not by forming a discrete and coherent statement of Hamlet's feelings about himself, but by taking us back into the play. We are in possession of possibilities of meaning, not certainties, and it is these possibilities which propel our attention forward into the play.

Look now at the famous 'To be or not to be' soliloquy in III.2.56–90. Read it carefully in the light of the work you have just done and identify how this soliloquy is similar to and how it is different from the first one. As in other speeches we have looked at, we can find a key to the function and meaning of this speech in its general structure, although here we do not have a disjointed, interrupted expression of feeling, but something quite different. How would you describe the relation between the form of this soliloquy and its content?

In the most basic terms, it is a reflective speech, and we can tell this even if we do not fully comprehend what Hamlet is reflecting upon, by noticing how the speech moves by gradual steps, one idea providing the connection for the next one. As we grasp it we can trace the source of each new idea within a phrase or a word in a previous thought. Finally, the soliloquy, which is concerned with the problem of 'doing' as opposed to 'suffering', acts out its own subject matter: thinking out the question 'To be or not to be' results in the very stalemate Hamlet claims thought will produce if one chooses to consider action rather than taking it. Thought and action become mutually exclusive. Three times Hamlet repeats and embellishes this conclusion in lines 83–8: 'Thus conscience does make cowards of us all'. Why 'cowards'? Doesn't this shift the level of Hamlet's discourse from more abstractly metaphysical to ethical and personal grounds?

Look briefly back to 'O, what a rogue and peasant slave am I!' (II.2.547–604). How do you relate the question of cowardice to both soliloquies? Is Hamlet simply repeating himself?

In II.2 Hamlet accuses himself of cowardice. His answer to his own question, 'Am I a coward?' can only be 'What else?' if he 'can say nothing',

> . . . no, not for a king
> Upon whose property and most dear life
> A damned defeat was made . . .   (II.2.566–8)

He precisely links that inaction to cowardice and to his propensity to indulge in language rather than action. Notice how the rhythms and stresses of lines 577–9,

> . . . Bloody, bawdy villain!
> Remorseless, treacherous, lecherous, kindless villain!
> O, vengeance!

are almost exuberant in the pressure of name-calling they accumulate, until Hamlet stops short and reflects again, 'Why what an ass am I'. When he becomes more reflective in 'To be or not to be', the content is not all that different, but the form of the soliloquy shows its concern turning from the strictly personal interest of the previous soliloquy to more general, philosophical questions about human values. Hamlet's restatement of the original question, 'To be or not to be', adds the qualifying word 'nobler', no longer making the relation between words and deeds merely a question of Hamlet's personal incapacities, but making the relation between action and honour a central issue. In this way, a general philosophical and ethical question becomes explicitly linked to the central dramatic question, 'Will Hamlet fulfil the ghost's command?' We no longer may merely ask, 'Will he do it?' but must also ask, 'Will it be an honourable act?'

At this point where the philosophical and dramatic problems clearly come together, the questions of the relationship between thoughts and deeds, between action and the role of language in evaluating it, become ones of which we, as audience, are made increasingly aware and at the same time conscious of an even more challenging way in which language operates in the play. The growing concerns of Hamlet's soliloquies reveal central questions we must inevitably engage with through our experience of the whole play: can 'honour' only exist satisfactorily as an idea; can it actually be realized through 'doing'? Can one guarantee the 'nobility' of one's actions? What happens if one's consciousness is at odds with the values of the world which challenges one to act according to its idea of honour? Is it possible for 'nobility' to exist in 'suffering' rather than in 'doing'? As Hamlet becomes more aware of the conflict between thinking and acting, we become more aware that Shakespeare not only uses language to tell us what is going on in the play, but uses the play to raise questions about the very nature and limitations of language.

The language of Hamlet, and of *Hamlet*, does not simply inform us of the events and characters of the play but becomes one side of a question about human experience the play itself explores: is language essentially in opposition to, irreconcilable with, action?

With regard to this central question, you might like to take time at some point to consider on your own the many implications arising from the play's use of 'acting'—that is, play-acting—as a metaphor. For a start, you can explore the resonances arising from puns on the verb 'to act'. And look again carefully at the way the soliloquy in II.2.546–603, introduces the relation between play-acting as simulation and action in 'real' life which Hamlet must decide to take. Think of the way words and actions are essentially interrelated within a play and how this contrasts with the problem of taking the kind of action which has been demanded of Hamlet. How do the many metaphors of acting illuminate the sense of irreconcilability between language and action that Hamlet expresses in his soliloquies? Does the relationship between language and action within an art form make us see that same relationship in life in a particular way? Think about these questions, too, with relation to the points about theatre and life which Roger Day brings up earlier in this block (pages 13 and 15).

Bearing in mind these issues about the relation between word and deed and the question of honour, look now at IV.4.32–66, Hamlet's soliloquy before he embarks for England and sets in motion the train of events which will end in his death.

First, note the main assertions Hamlet uses to encourage himself, giving this speech more than any other the tone and urgency of a personal 'pep' talk.

I came up with the following list:

(1) 'I have plenty of examples I could cite to urge me to get on with the job of avenging my father's murder.'

(2) 'Fortinbras and his army marching against a tiny patch of Polish ground present me with just such an example.'

(3) 'There is no explanation for my inaction when I consider my immediate and compelling personal reasons and the example of Fortinbras, whose action seems based on mere fantasy by comparison.'

As a result of this reasoning, Hamlet concludes, 'O, from this time forth, /My thoughts be bloody, or be nothing worth.'

What I have omitted are the justifications Hamlet introduces in lines 33–6 and 53–6. Look at these lines again and connect them with any key ideas we have encountered in previous soliloquies.

The idea expressed in lines 33–6 seems to connect to Hamlet's reference to his mother in I.2, 'a beast that wants discourse of reason/Would have mourned longer' (I.2.150–1). The Arden edition of *Hamlet* contains a note referring to the phrase 'wants discourse of reason', which makes clear its connection to the soliloquy in IV.4:

> The faculty of reason was traditionally recognized as the crucial difference between man and beasts . . . It was through his reason that man could perceive the relation of cause and effect and thus connect past and future, whereas the beast, precisely because it lacks reason, must live largely in the present moment.
>
> (*Hamlet*, Arden edition, ed. Harold Jenkins, pp. 438–9)

See also page 17 where Roger Day further discusses the importance of reason in *Hamlet*. In IV.4, Hamlet's phrase to 'look before and after' precisely contains that sense that reason–thought–language are responsible for the human capacity to relate cause to effect, the past to the future. It is the opposition between man and beast, created by man's possession of reason, which leads to Hamlet's second generalization in lines 39–44 about the relation of action to thought: either I am a beast and cannot reflect and see why the past urges me to take the required future action, or I am *too* human and my tendency to consider the nature and consequences of such action prevents me from acting at all. This conclusion, with its explicit reference to cowardice, echoes the end of 'To be or not to be':

> And thus the native hue of resolution
> Is sicklied o'er with the pale cast of thought,
> And enterprises of great pitch and moment
> With this regard their currents turn awry,
> And lose the name of action.

(III.1.84–8)

In the soliloquy in IV.4, Hamlet's attention—even his admiration—is drawn to just such an example of 'enterprises of great pitch and moment', and he links that example to the crucially defining factor he introduced in 'To be or not to be', the question of the relation between action and honour, IV.4.53–6:

> . . . Rightly to be great
> Is not to stir without great argument,
> But greatly to find quarrel in a straw
> When honour's at the stake . . .

In lines 47–65 he considers the example of Fortinbras, formulates a general proposition about the reaction between 'greatness' and action, which hinges on the question of honour, and then tests himself against this proposition and finds himself wanting. In television programme 7 you can see how this soliloquy presents the actor with difficulties which arise from the need first, to decide what Hamlet himself is saying, and second, what relation that meaning has to his subsequent action and, finally, to our understanding of the play as a whole.

Listening to different performances of the soliloquy can often more readily provoke us into recognizing the issues at stake than a silent reading can. Listen, for example, to the performance of this speech on Cassette 6(p), side A and compare it with David Yelland's performance in the television programme. What do the tone, pacing, and emotional level of these performances tell us about the way the actor understands his character and the dramatic context of the soliloquy?

In our own consideration of the soliloquy, one important question we must ask is whether our response to Hamlet's conclusion is at one with his? Does the language of the soliloquy take us along with it, so that we identify with Hamlet and agree with his evaluation? I ask this question, not because there is an easy or obvious answer—there may be no fully satisfactory answer, or many of us may disagree— but because to seek an answer is to question carefully our response to the play and to be drawn back into paying attention to the language Hamlet uses, to ask if our experience is fully accounted for in terms of a sympathetic response to Hamlet, the character.

Follow up this point by referring back to lines 47–56 and noting if there are any aspects of Hamlet's language which you found disconcerting.

The language which troubles me, and which I cannot simply accept without questioning some of its implications, includes Hamlet's description of Fortinbras in line 48 as a 'delicate and tender prince'. Can you think why? Look back at

Horatio's and Claudius's descriptions of Fortinbras in I.1 and I.2. I am also not sure how to read Hamlet's description of Fortinbras as 'with divine ambition puffed'. It has been suggested that this reference is ironic. Does that mean that Hamlet's reference to Fortinbras as a 'delicate and tender prince' is also ironic? The difficulty I find with the tone of Hamlet's speech here also affects my reading of his reference to the land Fortinbras is fighting for as an 'eggshell', and to his concluding, almost triumphant, claim that 'rightly to be great' is 'greatly to find quarrel in a straw when honour's at the stake'. I cannot read these last references as ironically intended, since they form the basis upon which Hamlet decides that his future thoughts must be 'bloody or be nothing worth'. The trouble I have with these aspects of the soliloquy underlines the way language can so easily slide out of control, how an idea such as 'honour', for example, cannot be fixed by a single, coherent, definition. Indeed Hamlet's reference to objects involving honour in terms of 'eggshells' and 'straws' calls attention to the fact that questions of honour cannot be explained in terms of the actual things to which they are made to correspond. The patch of ground which Fortinbras fights for in the name of 'honour' does not possess qualities which are inherent in the word 'honour' any more than an 'eggshell' does. Even the fragility of the eggshell emphasizes the essential instability of a concept like 'honour', as does the word 'straw', which is worthless in itself, its value depending solely upon the thing it is made to represent. Hamlet seems to recognize both the irony that 'straws' can be made questions of honour *and* that in order to act honourably, one must be willing to accept such definitions.

In previous soliloquies, Hamlet's tendency to reflect 'too precisely on th' event' tended to prevent him from acting at all. The slippery way his language works in his soliloquy in IV.4 seems necessary in order to propel him into action, but it also divides our consciousness from his. We as thinking, judging audience, may find it less easy to identify with Hamlet when we consider the problems arising from the language he uses. It is as though the lessons of 'thinking precisely on the event' are now ours to use in reflecting on our experience of the play. If 'nobility' and 'honour' are words which are appropriate for us to use with reference to the play, they may come to be defined differently from the way they are understood by any one person within the play, including Hamlet himself.

I would like you now to look at two sections of Act V and to think about the resonant meanings of honour when you relate them to the larger context of the play and the various aspects of language we have been considering. First look at V.2.1–72, where Hamlet tells Horatio about the events we do not see, but which 'took place', as it were, after Hamlet's last soliloquy.

Consider both Hamlet's language and Horatio's response. Do you find it a straightforward scene, sufficiently accounted for in terms of its overt function to fill us in on events offstage, or to explain and justify Hamlet's actions?

I am not going to give you a full account of my reading, but in working out your own responses, you might consider the implications of the following observations:

(1) Hamlet relates his actions to Horatio; we do not see them and therefore cannot judge them for ourselves.

(2) Horatio says very little. What interpretation might you put on this silence: deference, non-commitment, implicit consent or criticism, incomprehension?

The last section I would like you to think about is that portion of the final act, V.2.338–80, from 'O, God, what a wounded name', to Horatio's line, 'All this can I truly deliver'. Some productions of *Hamlet* end with Horatio's speech, line 353–4,

> Now cracks a noble heart. Good night, sweet Prince,
> And flights of angels sing thee to thy rest!

What effect would such a decision have on your understanding of the play?
How would your concern with the function of language in the play be affected
by a decision which omits the rest of Horatio's role, especially lines 368–79?

You may find some of the following questions helpful when considering this
larger question. When Hamlet says to Horatio, 'What a wounded name, /Things
standing thus unknown, shall I leave behind me', and asks of him:

> Absent thee from felicity awhile,
> And in this harsh world draw thy breath in pain
> To tell my story

do we assume, as we consider the events of that 'story', that it will mirror the
story Hamlet believes he has acted out? When Horatio says, 'And let me speak to
th' yet unknowing world /How these things came about', are we confident that
what he has to say will be the same as that Hamlet would have him tell? Finally,
is our feeling for Hamlet's personal fate, our wish, like Horatio's to call him a
'noble' prince, qualified by other aspects of language in this scene? Does Horatio's
speech, lines 374–9,

> . . . So shall you hear
> Of carnal, bloody, and unnatural acts,
> Of accidental judgements, casual slaughters,
> Of deaths put on by cunning and forced cause,
> And, in this upshot, purposes mistook
> Fallen on th' inventors' heads. All this can I
> Truly deliver.

substantiate or disturb the meaning of 'noble' as he uses it when he says, 'Now
cracks a noble heart'?

Look at the list of actions Horatio promises to relate and note the fact that
the metre slightly stresses the word 'slaughter' by adding an extra syllable to
the line, and the word 'truly', by putting the stress on the first syllable which
would normally be unstressed. What effect does the emphasis on these two
words have?

'Slaughter' is a word we normally reserve for the killing of animals or men in
battle. Beasts are slaughtered. When we apply the word to human beings we
stress the unreflective, beast-like action of killing. Relate this idea to other
references in the play about human reason distinguishing man from beasts. Doesn't
it seem likely that Hamlet, being worried about his 'name', would not wish his
actions to be described as 'slaughters'? Even his reference to 'self-slaughter'
(I.2.132) suggests an awareness that suicide is prohibited on grounds of the distinct
sacredness of *human* life, a distinction which slaughter in battle implicitly ignores.

Anne Barton, in the introduction to the set text, solves the problems posed
by Horatio's speech by concluding that

> Horatio astonishes us by leaving out everything that seems important,
> reducing all that is distinctive about this play to a plot stereotype.
> Although his tale is, on one level, accurate enough, it is certainly not
> Hamlet's 'story'.
>
> (Set text, Introduction, p. 52)

But does it not, at the same time, form a *true* part of Hamlet's story? He is as
truly implicated in this list as anyone else; it is no more possible to exclude Hamlet
or disregard his responsibility as an actor of these deeds than to omit Claudius

from the list. The death of Polonius was a 'casual slaughter', brought about by 'accidental judgement' and the deaths of Rosencrantz and Guildenstern were 'put on by cunning and forced cause' even as Claudius's murder of King Hamlet was. We recognize both that Hamlet's story is *more* than this list, and that his own acts are inextricably embedded in it. Anne Barton sees Horatio's list as a reduction, but it also serves to highlight a central problem the play makes us consider: the relation between actions and the language we use to evaluate them. Horatio's speech makes us aware that our feelings about Hamlet's nobility, our fullest sympathy with Horatio's words, 'now cracks a noble heart'—are accompanied by an equal awareness that such nobility must be qualified by, and may not ultimately be reconcilable with, the actions Hamlet has committed.

Roger Day has suggested that 'Hamlet appears to die without losing his honour or the sympathy of the audience, (p. 30 above). There seems no doubt that Hamlet gets our fullest sympathy, but it seems equally clear that Hamlet's fate, indeed the play itself, requires us to ask, 'Where precisely does honour reside?' The meaning and function of this one word 'honour' becomes part of what the play itself explores. Our fullest awareness of the relationship between language and action in the play makes us deeply sympathetic with Hamlet, the character, but no less conscious of the trap he has inevitably been caught in by the necessity to act rather than merely to speak. With his final words, 'The rest is silence', Hamlet seems to acknowledge that there is a point beyond which actions leave no more room for speech. The paradox for us is that the play—the finely worked artifice of words and actions—makes us ponder the limits of language itself.

SM

 *Forum*

The question of Hamlet's possible development

Why is *Hamlet*, of all Shakespeare's plays, the most talked about and written about? Is it that, as Graham Martin suggests, it is an imperfect work of art in spite of having as hero the most civilized, intellectual, self-examining and yes, most lovable human being in all the thirty-seven plays? Or is it that, by the usual processes of textual exegesis and active dramatic exploration, it is possible to establish what seem to be certainties—motivation for particular states of mind or action— only to discover that those 'certainties' do not, when added together in sequence, satisfactorily explain the character as a whole? Every actor of the part, and every director, has to 'take a line' when preparing the play for performance; and while that is true of every play, when it is done with *Hamlet*, there seems to be more opportunity than with other plays for critics to complain of what has been left out of the production. 'Where was the melancholy Hamlet in Mr X's playing? The procrastinating Hamlet of Coleridge and Laurence Olivier? The noble prince? The proto-Marxist democrat? The neurotic sufferer from the Oedipus complex? The conscience-stricken humanitarian? The *alter ego* of modernity's ideal man? The intrepid avenger?'

For structurally, *Hamlet* is a revenge play, whatever other related matters and themes go to compose it. Hamlet the Prince is the avenger-designate at the start of the action, and the successful avenger at the end. In a play on such a subject, in which Claudius, the proposed quarry, is so far-seeing, wily and powerful, it is not surprising that the events should turn out to be much as Horatio describes them to Fortinbras and the English ambassadors as they stand amid the litter of bodies:

> . . . So shall you hear
> Of carnal, bloody, and unnatural acts,

Of accidental judgements, casual slaughters,
Of deaths put on by cunning and forced cause,
And, in this upshot, purposes mistook
Fallen on th' inventors' heads . . .

(V.2.374–9)

Since revenge (the apparent intention of Hamlet from start to finish) and death (the possibility of which must be ever-present during such a pursuit) are constant factors in the play, it might be revealing of any development in the hero to see when and how Hamlet refers to them at successive stages in the action. Such a minor quest might help to clarify some of the larger questions posed above.

What a character says should always—one might say can only—be considered in its strict dramatic context. But there is a serious limitation in what I propose: I ask for explicit reference only, though implicit references might be just as important and revealing. For example, Hamlet's recital to the First Player of the slaughter of Priam by Pyrrhus, in which the Prince chooses and then re-lives the experience of a young man (like himself) killing an older man (like Claudius) plainly could be connected with his own wish for revenge.

Bearing in mind that limitation, which I impose merely to limit the work, and remembering that to trace through the play any other constant important to Hamlet (such as his feelings for Ophelia, or concern for his mother's virtue) might yield similar results, consider these thirteen speeches of Hamlet—six about revenge and seven about death, mentally noting the situation and circumstances in which the words are spoken, and interpreting as you go along. If your time is limited, pause for detailed thinking only at the references marked with asterisks. Write notes on these, or on those which interest you most, whether they are asterisked or not. But in any case, consider closely at least one reference to revenge, and one to death, from Act V. When you have done that, read my comments, which follow in connected rather than note form.

Revenge

(1) I.5.29–31*
(2) II.2.546–603
(3) III.3.73–96
(4) III.4.107–10*
(5) IV.4.32–66
(6) V.2.64–70*

Death

(7) I.2.129–37*
(8) I.4.65–7
(9) III.1.56–82*
(10) V.1.75–110
(11) V.1.161–212
(12) V.2.74
(13) V.2.207–18

Revenge

It has always struck me how inappropriate Hamlet's similes are in his first declaration of his revenge purpose (1). Thought ('meditation') was of course traditionally swift—swifter than any action could be—but why does Hamlet go on to link the revenge intention with the other matter that is uppermost in his mind, love? Traditionally (again), feudal and indeed Renaissance man when swearing himself to revenge formally gave up all other impulses, including especially love. So perhaps the headlong commitment to revenge here expressed, as virtue (or *virtu*) required, is not yet as real to Hamlet as it ought to be. (2) is especially revealing of the way circumstance shapes motivation: the revenge intention is pure and fully acknowledged, but something prevents its fulfilment. What is it? Is it just that the avenger is really 'John-a-dreams', or is it that Hamlet profoundly needs absolute confirmation of the truth of the Ghost's accusation? Formally, especially as the speech ends on a note of positive conspiracy, the latter is the case; but it is the nature of this shifting, riddling play to involve its protagonist simultaneously in many considerations, whatever the state of the action, however urgent the necessity of the moment. You can apply that to (3) and (4).

(4) carries a terrible weight. Hamlet has only just received the proof he wanted, from the Play scene, from which he has rushed to his mother's closet. So you could say, objectively with regard to the necessity of proof and the state circumstances of the mimic performance, that Hamlet could not have killed Claudius before this last appearance of the Ghost. But there is in Hamlet's words all the long and pent-up agony of his circumstance—not knowing whether the Ghost was a 'goblin damn'd', or whether his mother was not only unfaithful to his father while the latter was alive, but privy to his murder as well ('None wed the second but who kill'd the first')—as well as his guilt. The irony of (4) is that such a clear pronouncement is made when Hamlet is being taken by force away from the ground of projected revenge; it seems that the discovery of Claudius's plot to have him killed in England is positively required before Hamlet's mind may be cleared and his resolution calmly set, as in (6). But the play continues a teaser to the end—because who could imagine a hero avenger saying such a thing and then making no move at all to achieve his revenge? Rather, he goes passively into his antagonist's planned murder scene, the duel. I shall offer a clue at the end of the next section, and that is all I can offer.

Death

(7), with its almost adolescent general accidie, centred on a deep feeling of out-of-jointness connected with his mother's behaviour and his own apparent displacement from the succession, fits the kind of man who responds with relief a few minutes later to the prospect of certainty and action (see my comment on (1) above). It is interesting that Hamlet's weariness with life is instinctively expressed in a moment of intense action and possible peril (8) as well as receiving full intellectual consideration just before his confrontation with Ophelia and at a time when the Ghost's revelations have become a part of his consciousness (9). Is it leaping ahead of myself to suggest that adolescence is still there, but being painfully exorcized by and during the rigours of action? Concerning (10), one of the marvellous things about Shakespeare's tragedies is the way in which, when all the chips are down, and all the forces moving on collision course to the denouement are clearly defined, a philosophic pause is provided, in which new and powerful meanings reinforce the action. In my view, the elegiac consideration of death of the graveyard scene (10 and 11) delineates a Hamlet who is further changing. Acceptance, stoicism, understanding, call it what you will, come into his recognition of how things stand and how he feels about them. The philosophic considerations of the graveyard scene penetrate the relaxed syntax of the last things Hamlet says about death before going to his own death (12 and 13). They are the words and the grammatical constructions of a man at peace, in spite of the foreboding prescience of 'Thou wouldst not think how ill all's here about my heart'.

There remains the riddle of Hamlet's supine inaction as Claudius prepares to kill him doubly, by sword and poison. Wilson Knight opines that Hamlet's revenge is given him by a sort of grace: Hamlet does not have to do anything, because his long-delayed—and may we say, long-deserved?—revenge just comes to him.

I think the structure of the action, in which one must think of the theatre experience and stage time rather than apparently objective changes of scene and realistic time intervals, clarifies Hamlet's changing attitudes and ways of expressing his thoughts about revenge and death. The play and closet scenes, which are continuous action and not separate in Hamlet's experience, provide the watershed. Having crossed it, Hamlet is satisfied about his mother and is able to think of her judiciously, as he now thinks about revenge and death; cardinally, between him and Claudius, the chips are down, and it is war to the knife. Hamlet's positive inaction subsequently, coupled with his judicious and calm demeanour—with the notable exception of his brawl with Laertes—mean to me that he has in some sense passed beyond his tribulations to an acceptance of death. This is a combination of a recommended medieval Christian attitude and a post-classical stoicism which Elizabethans took from their Latin masters. He is a very different person from the agonized adolescent of Acts I and II.

BS

Is Hamlet a successful play?

'Is *Hamlet* a successful play?' Perhaps you would want to reply to that question with Auden's lines:

> The question is absurd:
> Had anything been wrong, we should certainly have heard.

How could a play of such world-wide fame, which has pleased so many generations of playgoers, attracted so many brilliant actors, and been the subject of so much analysis from literary critics of wide scholarship and acute intellect, *not* be accounted successful? What could 'success' *mean* if *Hamlet* is to be thought of as falling short of it? Nevertheless, this is the question I want to press. I hope at least to convince you that it is not an absurd question, even if in the end you still want to answer with a confident 'yes'.

Hamlet is clearly successful in a number of ways. The story, however familiar it may have become, always seems to bear another telling. The central dramatic tension (Hamlet *versus* Claudius) as it moves gradually towards explicit statement, never fails to excite, and the skilful climax in Act V remains theatrically satisfying. We are glad to see the villain dead, and in the peculiar way of 'tragedy', the death of the hero also seems right.

Then, as Roger Day has argued, the play is rich in immediate interest: a good range of characters, a striking variety of tone (suspense, wit, theatrical bustle, pathos, surprise), with a pervasive 'philosophic' quality as well which makes it unique. But the issue of 'success' can be taken further. It has been said that a successful work of art always contains within itself the reasons *why* it is *as* it is. However initially puzzling, it appears in the end as self-explanatory, self-standing. If there are a few loose ends, they are not felt to matter. Formally speaking, such a work is wholly committed to the expression of its subject, neither over-honed by anxious fuss about formal perfection, nor in part under-developed, as if the author had forgotten about some aspect, or failed to allot it an explicable function within the whole effect. It is in this sense (so I wish to argue) that *Hamlet* is not a success. It is not an artistic unity. The loose ends are not marginal, but central. Its subject is, finally, obscure, and its form skewed, internally fractured.

The central question of the play, the question that, formally speaking, keeps the play moving is, of course, 'how will Hamlet execute his revenge upon Claudius?' Initial worry about the Ghost's truthfulness takes us to the middle of the play and the acting of *The Mousetrap*. Claudius's reaction to this proves the Ghost reliable, and lest there be any doubt, we are permitted to overhear Claudius confessing to the murder in his prayers. Hamlet then visits his mother, kills Polonius, and is banished to England, having turned down a chance to kill Claudius for a very proper avenger's reason: adequate revenge must not give Claudius the chance of Heaven.

So far, so good. Hamlet's delay, though it already troubles *him* (II.2), is entirely understandable. Claudius is powerful, well-guarded, Hamlet cannot act openly against him, and cannot refuse the order to go to England. But then (IV.4) we hear him soliloquize after his accidental meeting with Fortinbras *en route* to fight the Poles. And what does Hamlet say? Not, as reasonably he might, that because of the King's power, and his own mistake (Polonius' death) in giving

Claudius an excuse to get rid of him, the revenge has been delayed. Not at all. His speech is full of inexplicable self-blame that he is not as Fortinbras, that despite all the powerful reasons urging him on, he is both *unable* to act, and unable to understand what prevents him. It is the mismatch between this speech and preceding events, that makes us ask whether Hamlet, as a character, properly belongs within the suspenseful story of political intrigue that is the play's dramatic form. Such a speech becomes the basis for those many psychological probings of the unarticulated depths of his character (most notably Ernest Jones's Freudian account mentioned by Roger Day.) It may be that reading the play, rather than watching it, gives undue prominence to Hamlet's self-analyses. But can they be ignored? Can a producer just sweep their implications to one side? Hamlet himself tells us that he doesn't know *why* he has delayed his revenge, even though the play to this point, far from seriously justifying his question, has given ample reason for his delay. Is it not understandable that critics, in the light of the Act IV soliloquy, have gone back over Hamlet's speeches in earlier acts, endlessly probing them for signs of an incipient and inexplicable reluctance to act, and made *this* the true subject of the play?

Put briefly, my argument is that Hamlet as a character is too subtle, complicated, many-sided, too *overflowing* for the play *Hamlet*. He is a veritable bundle of loose ends, each of which leads further and further from the simple revenge plot which commands the stage. Hamlet in respect of *Hamlet* represents a severe case of what we might call 'Falstaff-itis'. It is not difficult to find Falstaff more interesting, more attractive, more perceptive, in the end more *intelligent* than the play which includes him. But Falstaff is not, dramatically speaking, at the centre of the *Henry IV* plays. Hamlet, famously, is at the centre of *Hamlet*, and equally, he is very much more intelligent than his *milieu*. That is why, artistically speaking, *Hamlet* is not a success.

T. S. Eliot, in an influential essay, proposed an explanation for this imbalance. Reflecting generally on the mysterious process whereby episodes in an author's private life are elaborated into the public stuff of his completed art, he suggested that with *Hamlet* Shakespeare had failed to achieve a successful transformation.

> *Hamlet*, like the sonnets, is full of some stuff that the writer could not drag to light, contemplate, or manipulate into art.
>
> (*Selected Essays*, p. 144)

This failure in the artistic process permeates the play, and its direct analogue is Hamlet's mysterious failure to understand his own behaviour. There, suggests Eliot, the matter should rest. It is pointless for critics to strive towards a unifying interpretation of a play which simply lacks unity, for reasons which—knowing as little about Shakespeare's life as we do—we can never recover. After all, Shakespeare is not the only great writer or artist to leave us with a work of undeniably impressive stature, yet by no means satisfactory. To continue to 'interpret' it amounts to a shadowy second-hand effort to complete what Shakespeare could not.

To end with a more particular point about irresolvable contradictions in the play, I would point again to the soliloquy which Fortinbras's expedition against the Poles prompts in Hamlet, in which he takes the Norwegian soldier as a model.

> . . . Rightly to be great
> Is not to stir without great argument,
> But greatly to find quarrel in a straw
> When honour's at the stake . . .   (IV.4.53–6)

But how can we reconcile this kind of reasoning—conventional Renaissance heroics, such as we might imagine Sir Philip Sidney uttering before the Battle of Zutphen, or some famous Italian tenor singing in a Verdi historical costume-drama—with this?

> ... Who would fardels bear,
> To grunt and sweat under a weary life,
> But that the dread of something after death,
> The undiscovered country, from whose bourn
> No traveller returns, puzzles the will,
> And makes us rather bear those ills we have
> Than fly to others that we know not of?

(III.1.76–82)

Hamlet the would-be Fortinbras has absolutely no connection with the Hamlet who thinks so seriously, imaginatively and generously about human life, and (the point needs stressing) about *kinds* of life which he himself would not need to live. We may, of course, forcibly suppress the contradiction by speaking of the philosopher-prince. Alternatively, we may note that Shakespeare, not exactly inexperienced in the presentation of complex characterizations, hardly seems to notice the staggering difference between these two elements in his hero. Shakespeare, in other words, participates in the contradiction. Partly he thinks quite comfortably in Fortinbras's terms, following the ethics of feudal militaristic honour. Partly, too, he thinks quite comfortably in terms of the revenge plot—how could he write such a gripping one if he didn't? But then again, he has other thoughts which break entirely with the Fortinbras mould, other perceptions of the world and of his fellow human beings. And the whole aspect of Hamlet that is deeply hostile to the Danish court becomes the eloquent and memorable voice of such estranging thoughts. *Hamlet* is the play, I want to suggest, where Shakespeare first registers his substantial disengagement from the conventional thinking of his time, from the common-or-garden 'Elizabethan' element in his creative make-up. But the disengagement was merely in process, the author only partly conscious of its implications, and the play that resulted remains a symptom of the process, rather than its artistic realization. For this we must turn to later plays, and it is in the light of their achievement that we pay Shakespeare no compliment by calling *Hamlet* a success.

GM

The limitations of Hamlet *as drama*

When a work of art has been avidly admired and discussed by audiences in several parts of Europe for a couple of hundred years, one is compelled to look for its strengths rather than first emphasizing its weaknesses. It may be that *Hamlet* is so famous because it seems to speak of, and speak to, the situation of the Western intellectual as no other play does. Some issues raised by it came to seem specially relevant as the 'intelligentsia' emerged into being as a sub-class, during and after the eighteenth century. In Germany deracinated thinkers and artists of the Romantic period subscribed to a cult of 'free will' (such will as a prince should have scope to express) while conscious of their own actual impotence in a fragmented and rather backward country. Russia was unified but much more backward, and was ruled autocratically: to a Russian intellectual such as Turgenev, in the mid-nineteenth century, Hamlet's indecisiveness might well seem to project his own frustration. Neither a German nor a Russian would have seen anything unlifelike in the mediocre court of Shakespeare's 'Denmark', sodden with drink and rotten with intrigue. In Britain, theatre was dominated from the days of Garrick to those of Gielgud by the cult of the 'great actor'. Shakespeare's longest and most difficult male part had obvious appeal under such conditions.

Hamlet is always an absorbing play to watch, not just because one will never cease to be intrigued by new solutions found by new producers and actors to the problems (including textual ones) which it must engender for them, but also because of the splendour of its speeches (whatever textual solutions are found—'solid' or 'sullied'?) and the elemental force of the situation which it projects: one does not have to be a Freudian to find matter of compelling interest in a man's relationship with his re-married mother.

That said, I must confess that I find *Hamlet* less exciting to think about than *Antony and Cleopatra* or *King Lear* or *Othello*. I'm now responding to a challenge from Roger Day to explain why, when it came to the point, I couldn't muster any enthusiasm for my original intention to write about Claudius and his role, and how I relate this to a general failure on my part to love this play as perhaps I should.

Briefly: in the tragedies which I've mentioned, the eponymous heroes and heroine contend with other characters of their own size. Enobarbus, even Octavius might act with flair, 'take over' and divert us from our response to Cleopatra and her consort. A strong Iago is as needful as a powerful Othello. In *King Lear*, there is a galaxy of 'star' parts. Edmund can woo and win the audience, or Edgar can make something remarkable out of his taxing role, the Fool can determine the whole effect of the play, and so on. But in *Hamlet*, there is no chance that any character except the Prince can come into his or her own. A production which cut Hamlet himself down to the size of the other characters would be quite clearly perverse and counter-textual: as would a lively Horatio, a sympathetic Gertrude or an appealing Claudius. Ophelia has to be a broken reed, Polonius has to be rather a fool. Traditionally, all these roles are 'strongly cast', excellent actors are sought out—but I wonder if anyone remembers a 'great' Gertrude with such thrill as that with which I recall Peter O'Toole as Thersites and Patrick Allen as Achilles in a Stratford *Troilus and Cressida* decades back, or Albert Finney's Edgar, Michael Bryant's Iago, from productions which were not otherwise wholly marvellous? 'Hamlet without the Prince' is of course proverbial. *Hamlet* stands or falls by one main part to an extent rarely true in Shakespeare (much more so than *King Lear*, I would say, though you might find this judgement surprising and disagree strongly). 'Denmark's a prison', the Prince says in II.2. It is easy enough to stage 'Denmark' as a kind of totalitarian state. But what a mediocre, sottish, uncharismatic dictator it has in Claudius. Can we take Polonius behind the arras very gravely, as the spy of a corrupt regime? We think Denmark a prison because Hamlet thinks it so, or claims to think it so. Granted the poor human quality of the jailers it is very hard to see why he can't pull it down.

Maynard Mack in his essay 'The World of *Hamlet*' (reprinted on pages 234–56 of the Signet edition of the play) makes familiar and plausible points when he praises the play for its 'mysteriousness' and for its handling of 'the problematic nature of reality and the relation of reality to appearance'. You might like to read his views and look for evidence there to contradict my simple assertion that I find *Hamlet's* exploration of 'reality' and 'appearance' less interesting and moving than Lear's because the 'reality' constructed in the latter play is so much more copious and vivid. If, as the Signet editor suggests 'one scarcely thinks of *Hamlet* as a play of action', despite the many remarkable events in it, is it not because the 'characters' involved, except for the Prince himself, are stunted and somewhat shadowy? The abrupt deaths of Polonius and of his two children can't move us very deeply (or, at any rate, don't move me deeply) because for all the positive human qualities they show, they might just as well be dead—whereas the passings of Mercutio in *Romeo and Juliet*, Hector in *Troilus and Cressida*, even of Eros in *Antony and Cleopatra*, can be made as poignant as anything ever staged, and Edmund and Goneril, in *King Lear*, have a force, however nasty, which can make their goings take one's breath.

Perhaps I have been exaggerating. But when T. S. Eliot found it problematic and disappointing that Hamlet's psychological condition lacks an 'objective correlative', I think he was responding to features of the play which weigh on me also. A man of undoubted intellect and courage who is constricted by the likes of Claudius and Polonius would seem to be short himself of important human qualities. You might retort, 'That's why the play is so good: Shakespeare explores with amazing brilliance the Prince's unhealthy state of mind. Hamlet's doubts and tangles take to the heights of tragedy something which we can recognize in our own lives whenever the "pale cast of thought" diseases our "resolution".' And reading or watching the play, which *is* fascinating, I would have to agree with you, while holding to my opinion that the mediocrity of all but one of its characters greatly limits the extent to which it can move me. It seems to me the least impressive of Shakespeare's 'mature' tragedies, which is not to say that it isn't very remarkable.

AC

Horatio's dramatic function

> Horatio, thou art e'en as just a man
> As e'er my conversation coped withal.

(III.2.64–5)

Horatio is often held up as one of the most admirable characters in the play, second only to Hamlet himself. Not that there are many admirable characters to choose from. 'To be honest, as this world goes, is to be one man picked out of ten thousand', says Hamlet. And what goes for the world applies still more to Denmark—'a prison', Hamlet significantly observes, where it seems that the only escape from treachery and double-dealing is death (and not even that, as Hamlet muses and the Ghost laments). Hamlet is continually struck by the contrast between fair-seeming and reality at Elsinore, where Claudius 'may smile and smile and be a villain', where the good-humoured Gertrude is false to her late husband's memory, where Rosencrantz and Guildenstern are 'my two schoolfellows, whom I

Act III, scene 2 66–97 from the RSC production of Hamlet *in 1966 (Photo: Holte Photos Ltd)*

will trust as I will adders fanged'. This pair and Polonius 'fool me to the top of my bent'. In this oppressive atmosphere, even the innocent Ophelia falls under suspicion: 'Ha, ha! Are you honest?' Hamlet taxes her (meaning, 'Are you chaste?') Against this background, the only 'honest' man among the leading characters is Horatio. Of living characters, then, Horatio stands next to Hamlet in honesty.

And in constancy, dependability, predictability, he stands higher. He will do nothing rash. He is 'not a pipe for Fortune's finger'. Hamlet's eulogy to his qualities (III.2.63–74) is well known; it is in marked tribute to these qualities, against the overall falsity of Elsinore, that Hamlet cuts off Horatio's deprecating interruption with these words:

> Nay, do not think I flatter.
> For what advancement may I hope from thee,
> That no revenue hast but thy good spirits
> To feed and clothe thee? Why should the poor be flattered?
>
> (III.2.66–9)

Moreover, Horatio's stoic integrity—'more an antique Roman than a Dane'—serves, as is often pointed out, as a counter-balance and a dramatic foil to Hamlet's own delaying scrupulousness and indecision. Horatio embodies the steadfastness and decisiveness that Hamlet admires and lacks. And yet this aspect of the contrast should not be exaggerated. Hamlet is not the sweet, melancholic dreamer of Romantic criticism. He is a man of sudden, precipitate, impulsive and violent action. He does, after all, kill Polonius, Laertes and Claudius single-handed. He arranges the death of Rosencrantz and Guildenstern with cynical relish. He grapples in shipboard struggles with pirates, he puts his mother in fear of her life, he is brutal to Ophelia, he wrestles with Laertes in the grave. In terms of fatalities, his crime record is far worse than Claudius's. It is in the sense of temperateness and rational *self-control*, as much as of purposeful action, that the model of Horatio's character is to be understood. Even so, Hamlet's unique superiority is never in doubt. Horatio, loyal, unswerving friend though he is, at no time establishes an ascendancy over Hamlet, whose dramatic stature as 'courtier, soldier, scholar', even when he is at his most hesitant, remains undiminished and heroic. Horatio never rivals Hamlet in our respect. Hamlet's moral authority remains unchallenged, notwithstanding the chain of catastrophes unleashed by his predicament and actions. Though the two have been fellow-students at Wittenberg, Hamlet is not merely a confused undergraduate (as he has been portrayed in some productions). He is a prince. 'This is I, Hamlet the Dane', he declares, as much a Renaissance hero as Othello or Lear, and like Lear, every inch a royal.

Horatio, by contrast, does not actually do very much. He acts as a go-between. He shares the watch at Elsinore. In general, he seems as much an observer as a participant in the action, something akin perhaps to the role of Chorus. It is in keeping with Horatio's important but subservient role, that at the end of the play, when his personal preference is to act out a stoic death, he yields to Hamlet's injunction to live to tell his master's story, to report Hamlet aright and testify to his tragic nobility. But why Horatio? Might not Fortinbras have been made to serve almost as well? The choice is significant.

Dramatically, especially toward the denouement (e.g. in V.2), Horatio can often appear rather a 'yes-man'—not in the sense that he deliberately adapts his answers to what he thinks Hamlet wishes to hear (like Polonius and Osric). But quite the contrary: in the sense that in terms of the machinery of the drama, he seems to be present mainly to confirm the correctness of Hamlet's observations about people. And this, I suggest, is a key to Horatio's dramatic function in the play overall: he exists as a touchstone of truth. In the doubtful world of false appearances that is Elsinore, where truth is difficult to discern, in Hamlet's mental world of intellectual doubts and hesitations, Horatio provides us with a fixed vantage-point of common sense, an objective standard of right-mindedness.

Compared, however, with other Shakespearean 'truth-tellers' (like Kent in *King Lear*), Horatio's role is complex. Kent's dramatic task is relatively straight-forward, because it is obvious from the very outset of *King Lear* that Lear's abdication from power and his treatment of Cordelia show an extraordinary want of judgement, and thus trouble is almost inevitable. So Kent takes us with him immediately. But in *Hamlet*, as the play opens, objective reality itself is in doubt. We feel a vague unease and foreboding. Francisco remarks that he is sick at heart. Doubtless something is rotten in the state of Denmark, but we are not yet in a position to say what. We do not know what to think. In this uncertainty, Horatio leads us through the action as a sort of guiding light, a faithful companion as much of the audience as of Hamlet.

Horatio is witness to three vital truths:

(1)   to the existence of the ghost

(2)   to Claudius's guilt

(3)   generally, to the accuracy of Hamlet's moral perceptions. Just as Kent (and the Fool) demonstrate the folly of Lear's conduct and his disastrous wrong-headedness, so Horatio confirms that Hamlet is right in his assessment of Claudius's villainy, of Gertrude's shallowness and the worthlessness of Rosencrantz and Guildenstern.

It is vital for Shakespeare to establish that the ghost exists and that what it says is true. With what dramatic skill, however, he leaves us in doubt and suspense about the truth of the matter. He does, however, convince us; and this is crucial. Were it not for Horatio we might be in danger of not taking the Ghost seriously. Gertrude, after all, cannot see the Ghost, and concludes that Hamlet is mad, when he tells her that *he* does. Bernardo and Francisco, on the other hand, mere men-at-arms, may be ready to repeat, and to credit, such popular superstition as the groundlings might swallow. Their account is not to be taken on trust. With Horatio, by contrast, we feel that there is no nonsense about him. He is prejudiced, if anything, against popular credulity. As Bernardo says:

> Horatio says 'tis but our fantasy,
> And will not let belief take hold of him

> (I.1.23–4)

Horatio is a scholar, a philosopher, by training and self-discipline schooled to use his judgement. He will not admit, unless compelled by the evidence of his senses, the possibility of phenomena beyond the immediate and the physical. His imagination, in contrast to Hamlet's, is sober and circumscribed. Hence the subtlety of his testimony. The fact that makes it so convincing, both to Hamlet and to us, is that Horatio is by nature the last man likely to believe in ghosts.

'What, has this thing appeared again tonight?' These are almost Horatio's first words (and surely they must be attributed to him, and not, as in some editions, to Marcellus). The emphasis is on '*thing*', the tone, is mocking, disbelieving, sardonic. Horatio, as Bernardo says, is 'fortified against our story', which he at first dismisses, indeed, as no more than a 'ghost story'. Much ink has been spilt on the question of how far Shakespeare and his audience believed in ghosts. What matters for the play is that *this* ghost exists. Or, at any rate, that some kind of apparition is stalking the battlements.

Even then, we advance to the truth by systematic, logical steps (and with increasing dramatic tension). Horatio agrees, first, that *a* ghost has manifested itself; second, that it bears a striking resemblance to Hamlet's father. He will not make the invalid syllogism that it *is* the ghost of Hamlet's father and that what it says *must* be true. On the contrary, he wonders whether it is not a malign spirit, sent to drive Hamlet to madness or death. The questions of the ghost's veracity and of Claudius's guilt remain in suspense and are not finally resolved until Claudius's own confession in III.3.

Likewise, during the play within the play, it is Horatio whom Hamlet asks to watch Claudius's reactions:

> Observe my uncle. If his occulted guilt
> Do not itself unkennel in one speech,
> It is a damnèd ghost that we have seen,
> And my imaginations are as foul
> As Vulcan's stithy . . .

(III.2.90–4)

Horatio's role again emphasizes not only his reliability, but, more important still, brings out an aspect of Hamlet's character. Hamlet's reservations are not only the reflections of a melancholic temperament. They are the scruples of a balanced and meticulously fair judgement. He will not jump to conclusions without incontrovertible evidence. He continues to give Claudius the benefit of the doubt, despite (and doubtless just because of) his own strong personal aversion towards him, and the powerful promptings of his intuition ('prophetic soul'). This is not cowardice. It is not mere procrastination, but a sense of honour and justice. In contrast to Laertes's rash and unscrupulous recourse to blind vengeance for the death of *his* father, Hamlet will *not* act in reliance on his own unaided judgement, still less on mere instinct. As a scholar, he too is trained to mistrust both.

In a striking reversal of the initial attitudes of the two men, at the end of the play, it is Horatio, the avowed sceptic, who cautions Hamlet to listen to his inner premonitions and avoid the duel with Laertes; while Hamlet, who had hitherto almost constantly doubted and delayed, now dismisses his friend's advice: 'Not a whit. We defy augury'. Both have learned in the course of the action, Hamlet a faithful providentialism, his friend that:

> There are more things in heaven and earth, Horatio,
> Than are dreamt of in your philosophy.

(I.5.166–7)
TL

Some views of the play

I F you find yourself returning again and again to the play, you may like to know that there is now a journal published twice a year devoted exclusively to the play and entitled *Hamlet Studies. An International Journal of Research on the Tragedie of Hamlet, Prince of Denmarke*, Vikas Publishing House Pvt Ltd, Vikas House, 20/4 Industrial Area, Sahibabad 201010, Distt. Ghaziabad (U.P.), India.

Hamlet, a Tragedie by Shakespeare

> But an indifferent play, the lines but meane: and in nothing like Othello. Hamlet is an indifferent good part for a madman, and the scene in the beeginning of the 5th Act beetweene Hamlet and the grave-maker a good scene but since betterd in the *Jealous Lovers*.
>
> (By Thomas Randolph, 1632)

From Abraham Wright's commonplace book, *c.* 1655, quoted in Shakespeare, *The Critical Heritage*, volume 1, 1623–1692, Brian Vickers (ed.), Routledge & Kegan Paul, 1974.

If the dreams of Shakespeare were to be characterized, each by the particular excellence which distinguishes it from the rest, we must allow to the tragedy of *Hamlet* the praise of variety. The incidents are so numerous, that the argument of the play would make a long tale. The scenes are interchangeably diversified with merriment and solemnity; with merriment that includes judicious and instructive observations, and solemnity, not strained by poetical violence above the natural sentiments of man. New characters appear from time to time in continual succession, exhibiting various forms of life and particular modes of conversation. The pretended madness of *Hamlet* causes much mirth, the mournful distraction of *Ophelia* fills the heart with tenderness, and every personage produces the effect intended, from the apparition that in the first act chills the blood with horror, to the fop in the last, that exposes affectation to just contempt.

The conduct is perhaps not wholly secure against objections. The action is indeed for the most part in continual progression, but there are some scenes which neither forward nor retard it. Of the feigned madness of *Hamlet* there appears no adequate cause, for he does nothing which he might not have done with the reputation of sanity. He plays the madman most, when he treats *Ophelia* with so much rudeness, which seems to be useless and wanton cruelty.

Hamlet is, through the whole play, rather an instrument than an agent. After he has, by the stratagem of the play, convicted the King, he makes no attempt to punish him, and his death is at last effected by an incident which *Hamlet* has no part in producing.

From *Notes on the Plays* (1765) in *Dr Johnson. Prose and Poetry* selected by Mona Wilson, Rupert Hart-Davis, London, 1963, p. 618.

Shakespeare wished to impress upon us the truth that action is the chief end of existence—that no faculties of intellect, however brilliant, can be considered valuable, or indeed otherwise than as misfortunes, if they withdraw us from or render us repugnant to action, and lead us to think and think of doing, until the time has elapsed when we can do anything effectually. In enforcing this moral truth, Shakespeare has shown the fullness and force of his powers: all that is amiable and excellent in nature is combined in Hamlet, with the exception of one quality. He is a man living in meditation, called upon to act by every motive human and divine, but the great object of his life is defeated by continually resolving to do, yet doing nothing but resolve.

Samuel Taylor Coleridge, *From The Lectures of 1811–1812, Lecture XII*, from *Shakespearean Criticism*, 2 vols., J. M. Dent & Sons Ltd, 1961.

The surprisingly new possibilities of language which make this play appear a turning-point in the development of Shakespeare's style seem to have their origin in the personality of Hamlet. The new language comes from him, in him it attains to perfection. The language of the King and the Queen, of Laertes and Polonius, although subtly adapted to their character, still treads the well-worn paths; it is less novel, because the people by whom it is spoken are not in need of a new form of expression—on the contrary, they may be more aptly characterized by a conventional mode of speech. But Hamlet's nature can only find expression in a wholly new language. This also applies to the imagery in the play. It is Hamlet who creates the most significant images, images marking the atmosphere and theme of the play, which are paler and less pregnant in the speech of the other characters. Hamlet's way of employing images is unique in Shakespeare's drama. When he begins to speak, the images fairly stream to him without the slightest effort—not as similies of conscious paraphrases, but as immediate and spontaneous visions. Hamlet's imagery shows us that whenever he thinks and speaks, he is at the same time a visionary, a seer, for whom living things of the world about him embody and symbolize thought. His first monologue may show this; the short space of time which lies between his father's death and his mother's remarriage is to him a series of pictures taken from real life.

From W. H. Clemen, *The Development of Shakespeare's Imagery*, Methuen & Co Ltd, 1951, p. 106.